MARRIED TO DISTRACTION

Edward M. Hallowell, M.D., and Sue George Hallowell, LICSW,

with Melissa Orlov

Married

TO DISTRACTION

RESTORING INTIMACY AND
STRENGTHENING YOUR MARRIAGE
IN AN AGE OF INTERRUPTION

BALLANTINE BOOKS / NEW YORK

Copyright © 2010 by Edward M. Hallowell, M.D.

Published in the United States by Ballantine Books, an imprint of The Random House
Publishing Group, a division of Random House, Inc., New York.

BALLANTINE and colophon are registered trademarks of Random House, Inc.

ISBN 978-0-345-50799-0

Printed in the United States of America on acid-free paper

www.ballantinebooks.com

2 4 6 8 9 7 5 3 1

FIRST EDITION

Book design by Casey Hampton

We dedicate this book to Sarah and Eric Meyers, a couple we met when their daughter, Sophie, and our daughter, Lucy, were born. Then, our son Jack, was born about the same time as their son Sam, followed by our son Tucker, and their son Chad. In the twenty years we have raised our kids together, they have become not only like second parents for our children, but wonderfully fun and kitchen-comfortable friends for Sue and me. In hard times they are always there to help us out, and in good times they are always there to join us and celebrate. In dedicating this book to Sarah and Eric, Sue and I not only celebrate our friendship with them, but we urge all couples to celebrate their various friendships as well.

Contents

Introduction

Have you found that it is increasingly difficult to get your partner's attention, not to mention affection? Are too many of your conversations devoted to bad news and toxic worries? Are you feeling a little lonely, even though you do (usually) love the person you're with? Do you feel as if many important conversations take place on the go, or via cell phone with its incessant, infuriating dropping of the calls? Do interruptions often abort your attempts to sustain a conversation? Do you frequently cram an hour's worth of dialogue into two minutes of blurting as you're rushing out the door? Do you feel a rising anger at your spouse without knowing why? Are you frazzled, even worn-out, when you're only halfway through your day? Do you feel as if communicating with your partner is like trying to talk to someone who is sitting five rows in front of you at a sold-out rock concert where you have to scream just to get the simplest phrase heard?

If you answer yes to some or all of these questions, you're not alone. Welcome to modern life, with its ever-expanding array of ways to "stay in touch" using technology and with its ever-expanding array of worries that come from knowing so much about so many terrible things that happen in the world . . . and that could in theory threaten you. Don't misunderstand us. We are not Luddites, lamenting the state of our new technologically oriented world. Being able to be in touch with world news and communicate quickly when you want to presents an abundance of opportunities and excitement. This "brave new world" is spectacular in many beneficial ways.

But it can make your love life difficult, and it can sabotage good relationships without your knowing what's going on, unless you're wise to the unique traps modern life can set. Ironically, if you're not careful, your ability to communicate in so many ways can actually confuse and corrupt what you need to communicate and thereby damage relationships even between people who like or love each other.

You may sense that people around you are grumpier than they used to be, but you don't know why. One reason is that many people are inordinately distracted, overloaded, and worried. It's impossible to be intimate and sustain a loving relationship when you're in that frame of mind. This book will point out how to avoid the traps that can sabotage love, and it will steer you toward a stronger relationship with your spouse or partner.

We live in a world that's radically changed from just a generation ago. Life now poses new, unique problems, never before encountered in human history. We'll leave the discussion of most of those problems to the economists, sociologists, scientists, statespeople, and computer experts, who understand them better than we do.

What we know most about is love. So we look at the problem of intimacy in today's world. What we—Edward (called Ned), a psychiatrist, and Sue, a social worker—are best qualified to examine are the ways in which our new world makes love difficult, and what you can do to make your love as good as you want it to be.

What distinguishes this book from other books on relationships is our emphasis on what's new and difficult now and on how patterns of intimacy are currently changing. Due to the tectonic shift we've seen in everyday life over the past decade or so, the patterns of how people get close and stay close are shifting, right along with the economy, the political balance of power, the climate, and the speed of communication.

While intimacy has never been easy, today's world poses novel challenges. So much is new: from texting your lover to finding lovers online to competing with an electronic device for your lover's attention to feeling in your marriage the new economic pressures of recession, downsizing, and globalization, to living with faster change and greater uncertainty than the world has seen since the Big Bang.

At the heart of the current context is what we call the modern paradox: *never before has it been so easy to stay in touch with so many people electronically, but rarely has it seemed so difficult to maintain genuine human closeness.* Our electronic world has simultaneously allowed us and forced upon us a kind of emotional insulation and isolation from one another. What started as convenience has turned into a kind of extraverted loneliness: our world produces a massive, daily exchange of dialogue and data while the people participating in it feel curiously alone.

In addition, the combination of global politics, environmental pollution, and precipitous economic decline has ratcheted stress and anxiety into the danger zone. It's dangerous to live with as much fear and stress as we do these days—one more fact to worry about! We find fear and stress everywhere we look, in ourselves, in our friends, in our colleagues, even in our children. Stress poisons intimacy in relationships by distracting us from the people we care the most about.

We have all had a hand in the creation of our new world, if only by our being swept up in it and hurried along. Think of how the daily details of our lives have changed in the past ten or fifteen years. When did you first own a cell phone? When did you first get over one hundred channels on your TV? How long ago could you not go to stores on Sunday because they were closed? When did you stop handwriting letters? When did you first use Google? When did you first start to feel overbooked and about to snap?

Then, just when you thought you couldn't get any busier or handle any more stress, the economy tanked. Suddenly, invisible people you'd never seen and never known stole the front pages, and you learned they were stealing from you. You read about lost sums of money too vast to comprehend. But you could comprehend only too well that your trust had been violated, your savings depleted if not wiped out, and your job put in jeopardy. With that, you felt a new surge of fear and anger—and another worry!

Love and support from your spouse or mate now looked more crucial than ever. Where else could you turn? But you hadn't noticed that this crazy busy world had made finding that love and support more difficult than ever. Everyone's so preoccupied and distracted. Who can pay attention long enough to love?

THE MARRIAGE BEHIND THIS BOOK

This book is a collaborative work. Just as the primary solution we offer is the power of the human connection, so the book itself grew out of human connection. For the moment, though, let me—Ned— switch to the first person to tell you a bit about Sue and me.

We have been married since 1988. She is my love, the best partner in life I can imagine. I am not an easy man to be married to (I'm not sure what man is), yet she has loved me every day and given me more than I ever hoped for in a marriage. She is the sanest, kindest, and most loving person I know.

She is also a master therapist. Her credential is an LICSW, a licensed independent clinical social worker. She has always been fascinated by people: how they get along—or fail to get along—and what can be done to improve their getting along.

Because I have attention deficit disorder (ADD) myself, Sue has become an expert over our decades of marriage in being intimate with someone whose attention is inconsistent. She has also made a specialty in her private practice of working with couples in which one or both members has ADD. Sue does not have ADD herself, but she jokes that on some days she wonders if it is contagious.

We also have three children, whom, of course, we infinitely adore. All three have ADD in one form or another, and helping them thrive is the greatest source of joy and satisfaction in life for Sue and me.

Combining my nearly three decades of experience in treating ADD as a psychiatrist with Sue's experience in working with couples, we make a perfect duo to write a book about distraction and its impact on relationships.

This book, however, is not about the impact of diagnosed ADD on relationships (though see chapter 11 for a focus on just that). Here we broaden the target beyond ADD to include all relationships in which distraction and worry play a role—which means just about every relationship today. Whether or not a member of a couple has officially been diagnosed with ADD, or an officially diagnosed anxiety disorder or stress-related condition, distraction, anxiety, and stress are so prevalent in modern life that some form of distraction interferes with every relationship. Having learned as much about attention, inattention, and worry as we have, we offer this book as a guide for all people who find that lack of attention, a crazy busy lifestyle, and toxic worry, are getting in the way of intimacy.

We have geared this book to help you achieve the following three goals:

1. To see clearly what you want in your main relationship and to feel every day that you are getting closer to that vision.
2. To relish your life in love.
3. To feel inspired every day by the power of your dream and the opportunity you have to pursue it.

The overriding message on our every page is a message of hope. Realistic, honest hope. You *can* take back control, at least some control, in this uncertain world. You *can* quell toxic worry. And you *can* have the kind of love you want.

Part 1

MODERN ISSUES IN
INTIMACY

ONE

The Anatomy of Modern Love

Praised be the fathomless universe,
For life and joy, and for objects and knowledge curious,
And for love, sweet love—but praise! praise! praise!

—WALT WHITMAN

You've picked up this book for a reason. Your concern is love.

You've likely hit a snag, maybe a small one, maybe large. Human intimacy is so complex, so coiled and convoluted, that it's hard not to hit a snag. Most of us hit snags all the time in our dealings with others, especially those we are closest to. So, if you've hit a snag, just hang on. Keep up the effort. Anyone who tells you it's easy to stay together over the long haul has never done it. If you're still taking it seriously and working at it, your efforts will pay off as long as you have a plan that makes sense. It's not enough just to take it seriously and work at it. Some people work at it their whole lives long and get nowhere. To help your efforts to keep your love alive and your marriage intact, we offer a plan based on what we know works best.

When a couple is in a good place, each partner feels secure and fulfilled. To feel secure and fulfilled in a relationship, both people need to feel:

- that the other person thinks highly of them.
- that the other person cares deeply for them.
- that the other person thinks they are proficient at something.

Beyond that, for love to become what we all want it to become, a smile should cross your face when you think of your mate. You ought to think of him or her as someone you have fun with, someone you look forward to seeing, someone who for an undefinable reason makes life feel special. You want to feel that he or she casts a glow into your life that makes you feel good, no matter what else might be going on.

When all goes right, a natural sequence of five steps leads to such happiness in love. Each step should usher in the next, but, as we will later describe, modern life tends to snag each one. The steps are:

1. Attention
2. Time
3. Empathy
4. Connection
5. Play

Love begins in attention. Love begins when you notice another person. Love starts with a catching of your eye. Be it on some enchanted evening across a crowded room, or via an ad on Match.com, some signal—somehow—draws your attention to one person and not to another. No one has ever figured out exactly why and how this happens when and where it does—but it does, and has done so since the dawn of time.

In today's world, distractions interrupt attention all the time. The basic prerequisite of love—attention—can seem impossible to give or get.

Once you have each other's attention—no small feat—the next

step toward love is to sustain that attention over time. Without sustained attention, love cannot grow. On the other hand, too much attention can snuff it out. While some people purport to know the right proportions in advance, each love is different, which is why there is no one recipe and why "prescriptions for finding love" offered by "experts" so often fail.

Giving and receiving attention becomes a kind of dance as love grows. Now you see me, now you don't. Playing hard to get. Don't be too easy. If you want me, you'll have to pursue me. At this stage, attention is often focused on the other in absentia. Resisting picking up the phone to make the call. Deliberately avoiding the other person while thinking about him or her day and night. Preoccupied by the other person, but keeping a certain distance. This is the dance of developing love.

Once again, our age of distraction can disrupt the dance. If you don't have time to ponder and wonder, if you don't have time to approach and avoid and put your heart into it, then love will falter here, not because you are a mismatch but because you have not created sufficient focus for love to grow.

Attention given and received in proper measure over time, a recipe that varies from couple to couple, leads to a deeper interest in and a greater knowledge of the other person, which constitutes understanding and empathy.

Mutual empathy creates a connection. It is impossible to overestimate the power of connection at its strongest. It drives life. But it cannot develop if people are unable to sustain attention over time. Such a mundane obstacle—distraction—ruins millions of potentially intimate relationships in our modern age.

But if you are able to create genuine connection, you've got it made. This is the great reward of love. In connection, you feel safe enough to become vulnerable. You feel safe enough to let go and to play. Play is the main action of true love. By play we mean any activity in which your imagination comes alive.

Play often begets its cousin, celebration. New research shows that more important than being there for your partner when times are tough is being there for your partner when times are good. The study found that being excited and happy for your partner when he or she brings home good news was a stronger predictor of the strength of the relationship than being stalwart when bad news hits.

Being able to play and to celebrate—being able to have fun together—are far more important than most people believe. They are a cornerstone of all great relationships.

As we have mentioned and will continue to show, the conditions of modern life threaten all five of the steps we've named, which in turn threatens the vibrancy and power of your love—not because you are mismatched, not because you are impaired people, but simply because today's world sets unique traps that can derail even the best relationships.

Of course, we don't know *exactly* how the help you'll find here will help you because we don't know the particulars of your situation. You may be in great distress, or just a little worried. Whatever the case, you probably want to get more from your marriage (or other close relationship) than you are currently getting. This book will help you in that regard. If you follow the suggestions we offer in these pages, it will be impossible for you not to develop a closer and more enjoyable relationship. And don't worry, the suggestions are not at all difficult to implement. You won't have to learn a foreign language or join a new religion. All you really have to do is set aside some time. Not easy, but possible, right?

You may believe your marriage is basically good, but it could use a tweak. Or you might feel like the person who once said to Ned, "I know my marriage is just fine . . . until I stop and think about it."

There is likely love in your marriage, and we will build on that love. But even if you think there is no love, we will help you search out what's positive. At the heart of our method is the identification and development of what's already good. You wouldn't be with your partner if you didn't once have love, or something like love, but that love might now not be so easy to find.

As one of Ned's patients once said, "My husband and I work so hard to get everything done, we're like a small business, and businesses don't run on love. Earn the money, take care of the kids, keep up the house, do the holidays and birthdays and celebrations, bake the cookies, do the school and homework thing, keep up with the relatives, you know the drill. With all there is to get done, I sometimes ask myself, 'But where's the love?' You know, like, get real, who has time for *that*?"

At times we're simply too busy to pay attention to the people we love the most. We take them for granted. There's just so much to do. You may be exasperated at how difficult it has become to get your spouse's full attention or to find some enjoyable chunks of time for yourselves together, time when you're both fully present.

Life has also become so insecure, so fraught with worry and uncertainty, that it can be difficult to connect romantically. You may feel as if you are handling one crisis after another, or at best, one worry after another.

We do live in worried times. So, you're probably not only looking for deeper love but also for greater stability . . . in a world where neither love nor stability is easy to find.

You also may be hoping for some fun. But today, fun often gives way to fear. As you read this, you may be wondering if any of the hopes we've mentioned are realistically *possible* given the frenzy and anxiety of modern life and all the stuff you have to do just to stay afloat. Marital bliss may seem like a preposterous pipe dream, not an attainable goal.

Perhaps marital *bliss* is hyperbole, but genuine joy in a marriage is a goal that we believe any person can reach. We believe the pipe dream is not preposterous. We will show you what you can do to overcome many of the obstacles marriages and other intimate relationships face these days.

We want to connect with you, no matter where you are emotionally. As we wrote the book, we always imagined your side of the conversation, your concerns, your needs, and we tried to anticipate what you might want to know. We've looked at marriage in a modern context, your context.

One of the most jarring facts about modern life is how angry, contentious, and unfriendly it can be. Thanks to technology, we live in an age of instant *gotcha!*—an age of nonstop gossip and muckraking streaming endlessly across screens worldwide, an age of disappearing privacy and mounting mistrust, an age of witty ridicule in which the clever put-down gets attention, while the pat on the back seems hokey and obsolete.

Yet, most of us would like a pat on the back as well as some harmony in our lives. Aren't you tired of exposés, fallen heroes, corrupt leaders, and broken promises? Wouldn't you like someone you can truly believe in? Don't look at the news to find that person. Look homeward. Look to your friends. Most of all, look to your mate. These days it is best to create your own safe haven, your own network of positive connections, your local protection against the storm of data and disappointments we call the news.

In addition to distemper, our age is unique in its unprecedented levels of distraction and worry. Our daily lives so burst with information and random, ominous data that for a fact, opinion, or idea to penetrate past our eyeballs and into our minds, it must arrive at high speed with armor-piercing barbs. Friendliness is too slow and unbarbed to get in. There's no "hook" to civility. That's why it's going the way of the rotary telephone and the handwritten thank-you note. We need noise, conflict, bad news, disagreement, another person's pain, even our own pain . . . *then* we pay attention.

As such rancor rises, many of us feel an unmet need for some kind words, but we hesitate to ask for them or even to offer them, lest we seem feeble, passé, or vulnerable.

Yet the success of marriages and all other close relationships depends upon slowing down enough and opening up enough to create a space that welcomes simple, kind words. Such words are hard to find "out there." We will help you find them and create them, wherever you may be.

Unlike the dream of getting rich, or getting famous, or winning the Nobel Prize, or making it to the major leagues, or living to the age of 110, the dream of love is a dream every person in the world can make come true. Don't give up on it.

If you've read this far, you haven't.

But you're a little frustrated—or maybe a lot frustrated—with your difficulty in turning your relationship into what it could be or keeping it where you want it to be. Warmth and intimacy require daily effort . . . but who has time? There are bigger worries to worry about than love. You resonated with the title, *Married to Distraction*, and thought to yourself, "Yes! That's it! It's that simple, but that difficult! If we could just make each other a priority . . . if we could just connect for more than a minute or two . . ."

You may be frustrated by your partner's tendency to disappear, literally or figuratively, in the middle of what you thought was an important conversation or project. You're probably wondering what in the world you have to do to hold on to his or her attention long enough to connect in the ways you so dearly want to connect. You may be trying to figure out how you, yourself, can be more mentally present and engaged with the person or people you love, while still doing all the gazillion things that you have to do every day. There's so much to worry about. Where can love fit in? Isn't love a luxury, a frill for the idle rich? (Lest you believe that, by the way, one of the few rock-solid findings in sociology is the *lack* of correlation between wealth and happiness. Once your income rises above the poverty level, increasing levels of income do not predict increasing levels of joie de vivre. Sure, we'd all like to be part of the experiment, but it's been done, and done many times!)

You may also wonder if you simply want too much from your marriage. You may say to yourself, "Maybe this day-to-day distance is what a real-life relationship is usually like. Perhaps I just need to face that romance is for fairy tales and real life is more like novels where everyone is unhappy and frustrated, and the smartest characters are the ones who accept the unavoidable limitations of life. Maybe the best I can hope for is to avoid disasters and make do with what I've got."

Even so, *you do want more.* That is a healthy instinct, not a greedy one. It is good to want the most from love. You don't want to give up on your dream, and you shouldn't. You wonder why you have to spend so much time doing grunt work, tending to the *chores* of life—from taking out the trash to getting people to where they need to be to paying bills to getting the dog's claws clipped—and have so little time to enjoy the closeness you desire in your number one relationship. You may feel that a feast is going on in the main room, but you're always stuck eating in the kitchen alone.

You may feel as if you carry far more than your fair share of the workload, and you're more than just a little bit tired of it. You want to be part of a connected team, not two people working in parallel. You want to enjoy the feast together. As well you should!

TWO

Your Attention . . . *Please*?

Love is not measured by how many times you touch each other but by how many times you reach each other.

—CATHY MORANCY

"Tell me again, honey, why are we driving to Target?" Jim asked his wife as he slogged through slow, serpentine traffic on a steamy summer day. Jim hated traffic jams almost as much as he hated humid heat. The Boston area has a lot of both. The conditions made it difficult for him to keep his mind on anything but the heat, the traffic, and his displeasure at having to contend with either.

"It's just so hot," Elaine replied, "and I don't have any really light clothes. The kids don't have any, either. Don't worry, it won't cost much. Then we can go find a pool."

Jim kept driving. Three kids in the back squirmed, poked, and giggled, as they alternately tormented and amused one another.

"Hon, you want to go to Target, right?" Jim asked, then waited for a reply. When he heard nothing, he repeated, "Target, right, hon?"

"Jim, I just told you I wanted to go to Target and I told you why I wanted to go to Target. Which part of that didn't you understand? Or weren't you listening?"

Jim stammered a bit as he replied, "I'm sorry, I thought I was listening, it's not like I was trying not to listen, it's nothing against you or about you, it isn't you at all, it's just sometimes I hear words but I don't get the information. This heat and this traffic are making me crazy. Don't take it personally."

"But I do take it personally. I take it personally because it happens so often." Elaine paused, then decided to go on. "What do I have to do to get you to pay attention to what I have to say? I know my life is not terribly interesting. I know it's not terribly interesting that I want to go to Target or why I want to go to Target or why I want to do anything, but to have you ask me over and over again where we're going right after I've told you twice, well, it's insulting. How can I not take it personally? What do I have to do to get through to you?"

"I'm sorry." Jim had been in this spot so many times before that the only strategy he had left was to take his lumps and repeat his apologies. He knew excuses or explanations would get him nowhere.

"Being sorry, that's just not enough," Elaine went on. "Being sorry is nowhere near the point. I don't want sorry. What good does sorry do me? You're sorry, but nothing changes. I know, this all seems silly, we're arguing over going to Target, but do you have any idea what it's like for me to know that half the time I speak to you I might as well be speaking to a rock?"

"I'm sorry. I try to listen, and I know it's frustrating for you. This heat and the traffic really put me in a bad place."

"There's always an excuse. I understand about the heat and the traffic, but I would be far more sympathetic if there weren't always some reason. Whatever the reason, it's almost impossible to get you to listen sometimes. It's more than frustrating. It makes me feel so alone. And what makes it worse, you don't really seem to care."

When we think of intimacy, we usually think of nakedness and vulnerability. We think of opening up and sharing our deepest secrets.

We think of revealing our true selves. But before any of that can happen, something else must occur. It is a necessary first step for intimacy, a step that used to be taken for granted. It is called paying attention.

At the very least, intimacy requires attention. Without attention, emotional closeness is impossible. Distraction is to an intimate conversation as water is to fire.

Paying attention *sounds* so simple. In fact, it sounds like one of the easiest of all mental tasks. Anyone can pay attention. You wake up, you pay attention, and that's it, until you go to sleep at the end of the day, right? Compared to, say, thinking up a new idea or even thinking at all, paying attention would seem simple.

But it isn't. It is especially complicated and difficult in the twenty-first century. In decades past, we took paying attention more or less for granted. But technology has changed all that. We have lurched, the older among us rather clumsily, into a new era. Not since Gutenberg invented the printing press has technology so radically reshaped everyday life. We live in the free fall of epochal change.

The "simple" act of paying attention is becoming arduous, like trying to listen to a distant radio broadcast that is filled with static, or trying to see the highway as you're speeding through a rainstorm without windshield wipers.

In our era of ubiquitous electronic communications technology, in our age that author and newspaper columnist Tom Friedman has called "the age of interruption," paying attention requires all your mental muscles to swim against currents that pull and tug in an effort to sweep you away from whatever you're trying to attend to.

This situation is confusing and difficult because it is new. Never before have we been *able* to ask our brains to process as many data points as we can today. Never before have we been able to do as much in the blink of an eye, in a flash, in a jiffy, as we can today. The techies have even defined a jiffy. It is one one-hundredth of a second. How much can you get done in a jiffy?

We measure our lives in jiffies because never before have we had so much to attend to. Never before have we faced as many decision points, second to second, as we do today. Every moment—every jiffy—we have a choice. Every flash offers a chance for diversion. In every blink of an eye we must decide what to pay attention to, what temptation to resist, what lead to follow, what knock on which door to respond to, and which to ignore. Each of us is an air traffic controller perched in our own personal mission-control observatory tower. Only problem is, our mental control towers, unlike those at airports, are open-air, ready to be invaded by anyone, anytime.

We are "blessed" with so many methods by which we can be interrupted that it can actually feel alien if more than a few minutes pass without an interruption. What did I miss? Am I out of the loop?

So accustomed are we to being interrupted that uninterrupted time—which was once deemed peaceful—can become oddly painful. How boring! Where's the stimulation? As much as we might complain about being interrupted, we still voluntarily if not compulsively check our messages—voice mail, email, texts—even when there is no need to. We search for an interruption and devote precious neurons to anticipating it, even when none comes. In the midst of working on a project or carrying on a conversation, we stop and check, not our progress with the project or conversation, but our messages.

Add to this techno-flurry the uncertainty and anxiety that beset modern life, and it is easy to see why paying attention takes more than ordinary effort. Let up for a moment, and the demons of toxic worry pounce. Will you have a job next week? Will your kids make it in the world? Can you trust your investments and your advisers? The list is endless.

———

What you're doing right now—reading a book—puts you in rare company. By reading this book, or any book, you vault yourself into the ranks of a dying breed of people who ponder and reflect, who actually do *stop and think*. Reading—or any activity requiring sustained mental effort—demands a level of prolonged attention that fewer and fewer people want to give, are willing to give, or are able to give.

Without noticing it, we are losing our capacity to linger and savor the moment. Reflexive impatience makes us rush, even when there is no need to rush. When was the last time you lingered over coffee, or savored a conversation, or took your sweet time in a museum or a bookstore? Don't you instead usually feel a compulsive inner pressure to *hurry up*?

But to love, you must slow down. You must pause. You must attend to the other person. Fast love is about as satisfying as fast food. For love to sustain you and give you the deep pleasures it can, pleasures that are unsurpassed in this life, you must linger over your love and savor it. What gives love its particular depth and flavor only comes through over time. The best love is aged love. The rest is infatuation. But to appreciate true love, love that does not alter when it alteration finds, you must take your time—not let it be taken from you. You must allow love to free you up from your worries and your hurry, at least for the moment.

To do so, you must pay close attention. You must look for the ever-so-slight change in expression in the person you're with, the tilting of the head, the movement of the hands, the sound of surprise at the latest news. For love to be the kind of feeling that it can and ought to be, for love to make all of life's pain worth enduring and to momentarily assuage that pain, you must let love engulf you like a luxurious, warm bath. Take your time with your love. Go slow. While you can.

———

In our fretful, speeded-up world, we can't turn back the clock to the days of Royal typewriters, nobody's-home telephone calls, or time spent alone without "electronic devices," as the airlines call them. But we do need to learn how to manage the chaos—and opportunities—that surrounds us.

Without knowing it or meaning to, we are training ourselves to be constantly on the alert for interruptions; to seek out messages incessantly, to process data rather than discover, invent, think, or feel, and in general to lose the propensity or even the capacity to ponder, pause, imagine, or give full focus to anyone or anything for more than a few restive moments.

Indeed, impatient and worried may be our national mood. Who can wait? Who does wait? Waiting is so yesterday. Today is hurry and rush. There is so much to do, so much to worry about. We have reprogrammed our nervous systems; now we *demand* speed. Speed is our national drug—not the street drug, speed, but the phenomenon, speed. As the novelist Milan Kundera put it, "Speed is the form of ecstasy that technology has bestowed on modern man."

Today's world is, above all else, fast. That's fine, indeed wonderful, as long as you understand the implications of it, the physics of it, so to speak. A new physics is at work in human interaction. Speed makes focus difficult. Going fast, it is difficult to pay attention to anything for more than a moment. If you're not careful, you can end up paying what Linda Stone, a former Microsoft executive, called "continuous partial attention" to everyone and everything. Nothing can grab your full focus. This is bad for business—and even worse for love.

When this new physics enters a marriage, you may start to feel lonely and resentful. You might wonder where the man or woman you married disappeared to. You might also wonder where your own life went.

Speed, overload, and anxiety have created an elephant in the room. But, unlike the other metaphorical elephants in the room that don't get talked about, when this elephant came into the room, it was a baby, our adorable pet.

Back then, we embraced our toys, our technology, with awe, love, affection, excitement, and surprise, if also a bit of trepidation—not unlike the emotions with which we welcome an actual baby into our lives. But this tyke then *grew*, as if eating some giga-chip recipe of mega-growth hormones. Because we welcomed it as our adorable baby, embodying our hopes for a better future, we didn't know what to make of its burgeoning size and its growing dominance over our lives. But now it sits there smiling, a full-grown elephant. It's time to figure out what to do with it.

This elephant is the force of distraction. It can dominate all our lives. The force of distraction pulls on us now as powerfully as gravity. Technology started it growing, but the mega-worries that have set in since the economy imploded have made the elephant huge. Worry is as distracting as interruption. Indeed, worry interrupts thought. It can lure us off track, divert us from our most important work and our most deeply held loves, and dump us into a daze of distracted despair.

How many times have you said to your mate or heard her or him say to you words similar to these?

"You say you don't have time to talk now. But you never have time to talk!"

"Will we be able to make it?"

"I'm sorry, I completely spaced out on that. What were you saying?"

"All I ask is that you look at me instead of that damn laptop when we're talking!"

"We're very busy all the time. But are we happy?"

"Can you please stop channel surfing and stick with one show?"

"I'm sorry. I know I forgot it last year, too. Please, please don't take it personally. There is just so much on my mind these days."

"I'm trying to be patient. I truly am. But I really need some kind of emotional closeness or I'm going to lose something important that I don't want to lose."

"If you promise and don't deliver one more time, I'm really going to lose it!"

"All this clutter. You might think it's no big deal, but I am totally smothering under it. I feel as if I live in complete chaos and it really upsets me!"

"Why do we have to fill every second of every weekend? Do we really have to do all this fun stuff? It makes it so that none of it is all that much fun, at least not for me. And I think we're getting the kids trained to look at life as one entertainment after another."

"When was the last time we sat down in the living room with a glass of wine, looked out the window at that birch tree, and just spent a peaceful hour together?"

"I love you but we don't have time to enjoy each other. And we never have time to work things out."

"The kids just want video, iPod, IM, and sleep. They're not developing any passion, any direction, any commitment. I think we're too busy to give them the guidance they really need."

"I have more to do at work than time to do it. Then I get home and I get a list with more to do on it than time to do it. That's why I turn on the TV. To make the world go away."

"Sex? What's that?"

"We keep saying we will talk about 'it,' whatever 'it' is. But we never do. I feel as if our relationship is being lived in anticipation of some breakthrough moment, but that moment never comes."

"I love you, I really do. But I hardly see you."

"We're under so much pressure to make money. It feels like money pressure has taken all the fun and spontaneity out of our marriage."

"You laugh at people who go see a marriage counselor. But I think they're brave. Don't you think we might benefit from talking to someone about how we get along and how we could do better? On the other hand, where would we find the time and the money to go see someone?"

"The kids are even busier than we are. How did this all get started? And how can we slow it down? There must be a way."

These are the kinds of questions we are hearing from the couples in our practices, the people who email us, the people we meet at our lectures, and the people we know as friends and colleagues. A new pressure has built up in couples, a pressure that always mattered but matters now more than ever because it has become so difficult to deal with. It is the pressure to make time for each other, the pressure to do what you really want to do with each other and your kids. Behind it all lies the pressure simply (but it is not simple!) to pay attention.

———

The more attention shatters, the more relationships suffer. This damage is all the more difficult to prevent because *most people don't understand what's really going on.* They can start to feel distant and annoyed without understanding why, then they do what we all do when we don't really understand what's going on: we blame one another.

But the root cause of this new problem often is not an issue of culpability. The cause of the problem is the new world of distraction that's grown up around us.

Modern life has turned people ruder than ever, less inclined to feel sympathy for another person, more self-centered, and less emotionally available, more data-driven, less aware of their emotional selves, more irritable, less able to relax and listen, more aggressive, less flexible, and in general more difficult to connect with comfortably. Unless we're wise to what's going on, we can become a grumpy group of busy people, full of road rage even when not on the road, ready to judge even when we know none of the facts, sitting on a ton of anger and frustration whose source eludes us and that we don't know how to make subside.

The impact on couples can be catastrophic—*but it does not need to be.* The passion that drives this book is the passion of knowing that there are solutions, that relationships can thrive today rather than falter. The passion that we feel in bringing you this information is the passion of people who've found out something vitally important, useful, and not widely known.

Without this information, people who love each other can start to lose their close connection, fight more than they ever used to, feel distant and disappointed, and see no way out of the situation other than to work harder and faster to keep up with all that has to get done. But all this working harder only leaves less time for being close with each other, which in turn leads to even more feelings of distance, isolation, loneliness, and anger. What was a good relationship can easily become a marriage on the ropes.

If this is happening to you, don't feel alone. Intimacy of any kind is in jeopardy in today's world. Intimacy has never been easy, but today, with so many different ways to deploy your attention, if you want to preserve love, you must

- insist on time with the person you love and make extended time for one another.
- learn to say no to desirable offers.
- get wise to the tricks of the multitude of thieves of your time and attention that swarm around you like gnats every second.
- have a clear vision of the life you want. You have to know what matters most to you, and you have to make time for that, with iron-fisted determination.

Here is a hard and fast Law of Modern Life: *if you do not take your time, it will be taken from you.* If you do not insist on making time for what matters, you will not do what matters. If you do not insist on making time for the person you love, you risk losing that person.

You may not lose the person to another person or to a career or to anything specific at all. You may simply lose the person's passionate interest in you and yours in him or her. Many are the couples who drift apart *simply because they were not aware of the power of the drift*. Without knowing it or meaning to do it, *they just let it happen*, losing each other to outside activities or people they didn't even care that much about. The drift of modern life is not always a drift; it can be a riptide.

You wake up one morning and say to yourself, "How did this happen? What's going on? I loved the man/woman I married, but what's happening now can't be called love. It's struggle. It's work. At best it's boring. At worst, it's agony. And it's certainly not fun. I've got this one life to live, and this is not how I want to live it. This has got to stop."

If you feel this way, you are not alone. *And there's a good possibility that neither you nor your spouse is to blame.* You might be the victims of the confusion and intensity that surround us. The solution is not to turn back the clock, which of course is impossible even if you wanted to. The solution is to understand and then master the new, unique vectors that slice through modern life and make it so difficult to hold on to true love. You can't stop the riptide but you can, if you work hard at it, gather the force to swim out of its way. Indeed, if you want your relationship to thrive, you must. But it does take effort.

———

No word for the force of distraction exists in English or any other language that we know of. It has never been the potent force it is today. Soon, we may have a word for it, much as the physicists invented the term *entropy* for the force that tends toward chaos and disorder. In this book we simply use the term *force of distraction*. It surrounds us everywhere we go, always keeping us in its sights. It can seem as difficult to overcome as gravity. But you must overcome it if you want to create closeness with another person.

As in the example of Jim and Elaine at the start of the chapter, inattention, though involuntary, can feel intentional and can hurt other people. Sustained attention is disappearing faster than the polar ice cap. The force of distraction is stealing our attention—and with it, the loves of our lives—all the time.

Maggie Jackson tackled the issue in her brilliant book, published in 2008, *Distracted: The Erosion of Attention and the Coming Dark Age*. Scholarly and compelling, Jackson puts her finger squarely and authoritatively on the issue so few people have named. James Gleick also predicted much of what we are seeing in his 1999 book, *Faster: The Acceleration of Just About Everything*. And Stanley Milgram, the great American sociologist, anticipated our overload and its various consequences in a prescient essay he published in *Science* in 1970 called "The Experience of Living in Cities."

The minute-to-minute allocation of attention has dramatically changed since the advent of our new technology. The force of distraction now rules. Years ago, we would eagerly check the mail, the snail mail that is, whenever it came, but it only came once or twice a day. We might look forward to it and pounce upon it when it arrived. But now that it comes all the time, every second or so, we can't unlearn our eager anticipation. Without knowing it, we have trained ourselves to look forward to our various kinds of mail even when we don't really look forward to what it usually contains. Some force in human nature seems to make an unopened message all but irresistible—leading us, indeed compelling us, to check our electronic messages reflexively, even when we know it is unlikely we will find anything of any urgency, anything of much excitement, or anything that couldn't wait, say, another fifteen minutes while we completed a conversation or a thought.

When paying continuous partial attention becomes the norm, brainwork suffers. We know about this in business, science, art, and any other activity typically associated with concentration. But it is just as damaging in love. Love is brainwork. Without sustained attention, love loses luster.

Just look at how frustrated the woman who sent the following email feels, simply because her husband, whom we'll call Don and who has long been a sound engineer at their local performing-arts center, can't sustain attention. While she loves him, she is desperate for help.

At first, I thought that Don was simply hearing impaired and needed a hearing aid. He tried that and found it unpleasant and returned it to the audiologist before our wedding. But now I think, while he probably does have some hearing loss (due to the loud music he is regularly exposed to at concerts), I think his problem is more an issue of distraction and not listening, instead of not hearing. Even when he is on the telephone, he says a greeting and often says, "Well, that's good," and doesn't really have an exchange.

When I tell him something, he will often hear my first comment and not wait to hear the next. For example, yesterday I took a nap because I felt like I was getting a cold. When I got up, he asked, "Are you feeling better?" I responded, "The nap felt good, but I still feel sick." He heard the first part, but not the second, so his reply was, "Well, that's good." I said, "Did you hear me?" Which has become my constant harangue. He said, "Yes, you said you enjoyed your nap, and then something else. What did you say?" I said, "I enjoyed my nap, but I still feel sick!" He didn't seem to hear it even the second time and I responded, "Damn, I wish you would listen to me." He didn't respond at all to that, so I'm not even sure he heard what I said—so I just walked away. I don't like nagging, but I don't like feeling unheard either. With friends, I am often embarrassed when Don responds inappropriately. I know he hasn't heard when he answers "Yes" to a question that should get a "No" response. His standard response to anything and everyone is "That's good." When we first met, I thought Don was such an optimist, and he is, but he also doesn't hear or pay attention to what is going on around him.

Don's problem has morphed into an epidemic. While a small percentage of the population, about 5 percent, have true attention deficit disorder in need of medical treatment, a much greater percentage of the population simply have trouble paying attention. It's not because they can't hear well enough, it's not because they don't care or they're depressed, it's not because they are selfish narcissists or passive-aggressive manipulators, *it's because their circuits are overloaded.* They deal with overload by tuning much of it out.

When you are married to distraction, as Don's wife is, your relationship buckles. When the force of distraction prevails, your relationship is in trouble. In the coming chapters we will explore what happens in more detail and what can be done to fix the problem.

THREE

Interrupted . . . *Everything*

Definition of a Bore: A person who talks when you wish him to listen.

—AMBROSE BIERCE

"Can we talk?" Joan Rivers used to ask at the beginning of her comedy routine. She had no idea how difficult it would become to answer yes to that simple request. Her heyday preceded the heyday of distraction.

Let me give you a quick illustration. On a day that I, Ned, had set aside to work on this book, I went up to my home office with my morning cup of coffee, opened up my laptop, and clicked onto this manuscript. As I started to write my first sentence of the day, my cell phone rang. I had made the cardinal error of not turning it off before I sat down to work.

Once it rang, I couldn't resist seeing who was calling me. Such temptation is a function of the force of distraction. Not only does the ring of the phone distract a person, but the curiosity to know who is calling adds to the tug the phone exerts. It is so difficult not to look and see! So I gave in. I looked. I saw a number I didn't recognize.

Now what to do? Maybe it was a wrong number. But maybe it was someone who needed me. Maybe it was a call I shouldn't miss. Here again we see how seductive distraction can be. Obviously, if I had set aside the time to write, and obviously if I usually turned off my cell phone during this time, I had arranged my life so as to reserve a block of time when I would not be reachable by the world outside. But distraction blinded me to this. Suddenly I felt indispensable. I had to answer the phone. This entire "deliberation" took place in seconds; I am drawing it out to explain the phenomenon. The power of distraction lies in how quickly it acts, in how it disarms our intellect and captures the primitive centers of our brains, centers we automatically obey before we have the chance consciously and deliberately to override them.

So I answered. Sure enough, someone needed me. It was the mother of a girl I was treating, and she had worried that she might not be able to reach me when she needed me, so I gave her my cell phone number, while also explaining that I would not always instantly be available. Therefore, I would have been within my rights, so to speak, not to answer the phone right then. But, having answered it, of course I felt compelled to stay on the line.

Here again we see the power of distraction in action. We see how it colludes with the part of me that wanted a prolonged interruption. Why would I want to be interrupted? Because writing is difficult! It is at times heaven-sent to have a reason to walk away from the keyboard, just as it can be heaven-sent to walk away from the brief you're working on, or the experiment you're running, or the engine you are fixing, or the intimate conversation you're having.

Once I had ascertained that it was not an emergency, I could easily have said to this mother, "I'm really sorry, but this is time I've set aside for writing. What's a good time this afternoon when I could call you back?" I know this mother well enough to realize that she would totally have understood. We could easily have had the discussion later on.

But, no. I felt compelled to stay on the line, even though in reality I had no reason to. This is the force of distraction in action. That external force, combined with the internal force, my personal psychology, created an unnecessarily prolonged distraction, which I blamed the mother for, but was in fact of my own making.

Years ago, before the widespread use of our current technologies, one of my teachers during my psychiatry residency told me, "When you get out into practice, you will find that some of your colleagues get called all day long and all night long. You might think of them as dedicated and devoted doctors. But the truth is that they get called so much because they want to get called so much."

At the time I didn't appreciate the wisdom in his words. I wondered if he was simply making up an excuse for his own unavailability. But now I know exactly what he meant. Many people want to be wanted. They create conditions that lead them to be interrupted all the time. They may complain about how busy they are, how much in demand, how little free time they have, but deep down they feel proud. They feel important.

Back then, when I was a resident in psychiatry, distraction was not nearly the force it is today, so it was not as simple as it is today to make yourself easily available. Today, if you subliminally want to be in demand, you can lose yourself entirely to interruptions without any effort at all!

After I spoke to that mother, sure enough, my phone rang again, and sure enough, I took that call. This time it was my car dealer giving me an estimate on repairs I needed done. The estimate was much higher than I had expected, so, even though the call only took a minute or so, it took me the better part of a half hour to regain my focus on this book.

Repeated interruptions lead to what we call the soufflé effect, filling up a given project with hot air so that what ought to take an hour can take all day. To prevent the soufflé effect, you must forbid interruptions, but the force of distraction can combine with your individual psychology to make you feel as if you *must* allow yourself to be interrupted.

In the example I just cited, the only negative consequence was that I didn't get the work done on this book that morning that I had hoped to get done. But if you take that example and extrapolate it into the world of marriage and relationships, you can see how, unless a person is careful, important conversations may never develop or only develop piecemeal.

The word *piecemeal* itself has taken on wider meaning than it used to. Unless we're careful, we now live piecemeal lives in a piecemeal world. Piecemeal conversations have become so common, and so irritating, that we use the phrase *cracked conversation* to describe a new, dangerously common kind of interpersonal exchange. To illustrate, let's say Joe calls his wife, Jane. Jane answers.

"Hi, honey," Jane says. "What's up?"

"I left a scrap of paper on my desk upstairs——"

"Wait a minute, honey. Jack, put that down. No, you can't take that downstairs."

"Jane, are you there?"

"Sorry, honey, Jack was just into a jar of mayonnaise. *Stop that!*"

"What?"

"No, not you. It's crazy around here. What——say——get?"

Joe could tell the blips in Jane's response were due to the call-interrupting service they had on their phone.

"Wait a minute, honey, this is Julie, I have to take this call."

Joe waits. He grows impatient. He wonders what he would do if the scrap of paper he needed were a matter of life and death. He waits some more. He starts to steam.

"Sorry, honey. That was Julie. She needs me to watch Tiger while she's away."

"Frankly, I don't give a damn about Tiger or what Julie needs."

"Well, there's no need to——me——your needs——I have to take this."

Now Joe is ready to hang up. But he needs the information on the piece of paper from his desk upstairs. Finally Jane comes back on the line. "What do you want?" she barks.

"I need the serial number on the piece——"

"I didn't appreciate one bit the way you spoke to me. Now you want me to do you a favor?"

"It's not a favor. It's information that will help me make a living, which benefits you."

"Oh, so I'm the one who just sits at home while you . . . Thank you, Josephine, I didn't see you come in. You can start upstairs if you don't mind."

"Can she get me the friggin' number while she's up there?" Joe asks.

"I've had enough of this conversation. You can get the number yourself," Jane says, then hangs up.

Moments pass. Jane and Joe steam in solitude while they ponder the next move. Who is going to initiate the call of apology?

He had no right to be so rude.

Why did she have to attend to Jack and take those calls? Don't I count for anything?

Where does he get off treating me like some kind of servant?

As for Julie, all she does is ask for favors.

If he thinks I'm going to call him back, he better think again. He can come home to get his damn number.

I've got to get that number. I can't drive all the way home.

Oh, all right, I'll call him. But I'll fix him later.

Oh, all right, I'll call and apologize. Anything to get the number.

Both call. Line busy. Expletives ensue.

Of course, this scene could happen without the interruptions, but it was the force of distraction that brought out the frustration and led to the anger a cracked conversation creates. Too many cracked conversations can ruin a relationship.

We still tend to focus on the content of what we have to say while taking for granted clear channels of communication. But that can't be taken for granted any longer, if it ever could.

Often the content itself is perfectly clear. Let's say it's not even conflictual, let's say it's something wonderful, like "I love you." If the channel to convey that content is constantly clogged, the content itself can quickly morph into "I'm mad at you." If the channel stays clogged, the content can easily become "I'm giving up on you."

The new challenge in the field of intimate relationships is to *find the time* for love, the time to develop love, convey love, speak love, even make love. What used to be taken for granted—time, clear channels of communication, availability, attention—is in such short supply that love can die.

The more cracked conversations you endure, the less inclined you become to seek out the other person. The longer love goes unexpressed and unshared, the less intense that love becomes. The more the expression of love gets frustrated, the less a person feels motivated to express it.

Intimacy requires more than sound bites. It requires time uninterrupted, attention undivided, and a commitment to forgo diversions.

You can take some simple steps to attack the force of distraction in your life.

1. Become aware of the problem. Radon is so dangerous because it is odorless and invisible. The force of distraction is so dangerous because it is ubiquitous and unnamed. So, name it. The force of distraction.

2. Then identify its sources in your environment. For radon, you put a detector in your basement to see what the level is. For the force of distraction, you need to use yourself as a detector. Notice, as you go through your day, what the chief sources of unplanned interruptions might be. Electronic devices lead the list in most people's lives. The answer here couldn't be simpler. *Turn them off.* Of course, don't throw them away, just learn how to use them selectively.

   Please don't protest, saying this is impossible. Difficult, yes. But not impossible. Learning how to restrict your use of electronic devices is like learning how to control your food intake, or alcohol intake, or any other potentially compulsive activity.

   Learning how to control your use of electronic devices is a special new skill required for successful love relationships in today's world. While your electronic devices may facilitate love relationships in some ways, in other ways they can ruin them. We know one patient who calls her husband's computer his "plastic mistress." He is on the computer late into the night, and by the time he comes to bed his wife is asleep. He is not having an affair, but he might just as well be.

   So, when you are having lunch with a friend, or your mate, turn off whatever devices you carry with you. If someone needs to reach you, they can reach you after lunch. In the evening, shut down work at a certain hour so you don't seduce yourself into working all evening.

3. Rediscover conversation. In lieu of surfing the Net or engaging in some other mindless electronic activity, talk with your partner. Talking can be fun. It can be relaxing. It can be foreplay. But if it never happens, relationships wither.

4. Set boundaries. One of the unique achievements of our modern age is the complete elimination of boundaries of space and time. The workday need never end. It can—and does—go on 24/7/365. But no human brain can participate 24/7/365. Therefore, it is up to the individual to create boundaries of his or her own choosing. But create them you must. Or, as our Law of Modern Life dictates, your time will be taken from you.

If you're not careful, your lack of boundaries can lead you into ridiculous behavior, such as the man we know who lays his BlackBerry down next to him when he makes love with his wife. Only when she threw the device across the room did he stop doing this.

Furthermore, as we will discuss in chapter 13, our electronic devices have so removed boundaries of space and time that liaisons and affairs have become far simpler to enter into than ever before in history. Sexual addiction is on a rapid rise. A conservative estimate is that 3 to 6 percent of adult males suffer from a sexual addiction or compulsive sexual behavior, which is defined as "inappropriate or excessive sexual cognitions or behaviors that lead to subjective distress or impairment in one or more life domains." It is likely a much higher figure, as people tend not to report the problem until compelled to.

The mere availability of the Internet, text messaging, cell phones, and BlackBerry dramatically increases the risk that a person, especially a male, will develop some kind of compulsive sexual habit that impairs his life.

Of course, this does not mean we should all get rid of our electronic instruments, any more than we should get rid of cars because cars lead to accidents. It does mean, however, we should take the risk seriously and learn to use the equivalent of seat belts. More on this in the chapter on affairs.

5. Learn to say no to good ideas, good people, good projects. One of the greatest parts of modern life is the availability of so much. From information to people to ideas, much more is instantly available to us all than ever before in history. But, as we are learning the hard way, you can have way too much of a good thing. If you don't learn to say no to some great possibilities, your life will be overrun by these great possibilities, and they will become like kudzu, choking out all that is good and valuable.

In future chapters, we will offer many more practical suggestions and pointers. Of course, no list is definitive or exhaustive. Best of all is for you to start thinking of your own solutions, tailored to your unique situation.

FOUR

Making Time to Connect

Only connect!... Only connect the prose and the passion, and both will be exalted, and human love will be seen at its height. Live in fragments no longer. Only connect, and the beast and the monk, robbed of the isolation that is life to either, will die.

—E. M. FORSTER

Loving connection is the most powerful force—*by far*—we humans can create to ease the pain of life and generate joy.

It is crucial to reduce the power of the force of distraction in our lives because the best elements of life—joy, meaning, success, health—all derive from a force that we call *connectedness*, a transcendent feeling that you're a part of some positive force that is much greater and more powerful than you.

The more you grow connectedness in your life, the happier, healthier, and more successful you'll be. Connectedness is *the* great key to the best life a person can live. And some unusual news: it's free and available everywhere to anyone.

You can create connectedness with a friend, in a family, within a community, on your block, with a book, with your work, with a piece of music, in solitude contemplating eternity or some idea or image, or at a party dancing with strangers, with a neighbor or cyberbuddy, within an organization, on a team, outdoors with nature, with a pet, with God or some higher power, and most notably of all, with your spouse. The more places you tap into the force of connectedness, the happier, healthier, better balanced, and more fulfilled you'll be.

Distraction erodes connectedness. The force of distraction, which derives from overload, interruptions, worry, and the other factors we have named, eats away at the feeling of connectedness. The more you contend with distraction, the less connected you feel. To illustrate the point, we offer a story.

———

Karen is riding in the passenger seat as her husband, Jack, drives. Chris, Pete, and Sarah, their three kids, sit in the backseat playing on or listening to various electronic devices. They are on summer vacation near the shore. It is a perfect day. The sun is pouring down, but it's not too hot. The salt air mixes with the smell of honeysuckle bushes as the family drives along a back road. They have packed a picnic lunch of tuna-fish sandwiches, pb&j's, potato chips, cookies, Gatorade, wine for Karen and beer for Jack, and they are headed for their favorite beach.

Jack is listening to a jazz CD. Karen is looking out the window, not thinking of anything in particular, drinking in the day. Suddenly, a chill comes over her, like a cold current when you're swimming in warm water. She braces. Tears come to her eyes, which she quickly dabs away so they won't be noticed. She is taken back to her own childhood, when these car rides were full of tension or out-and-out battles. Briefly, she sees the image of her stepfather reaching across from the driver's seat to slap her mother. From the backseat, she screams out, "Stop! Don't hurt Mama!" Quickly her mother turns back to her and says, "It's all right, honey, don't worry, it was my fault, I gave him the wrong directions." She hears her stepfather say, "Damn right!" She shudders as the memory passes around and through her, then recedes.

She takes a deep breath, then lets it out. She leans her head out the window and enjoys the fresh air for a moment. Then she looks back at the kids and she leans over to Jack and nuzzles her face against his shoulder and gives him a little kiss. From the backseat, Pete pipes in, "Oooo, that's gross."

"C'mon, Pete," Karen says, "can't I give your dad a kiss?" She feels almost giddy to be rid of that memory and in the current car.

"No. At least not in front of us!"

"All right," Karen says with a smile, "I'm just so happy. I'll save it for later."

"That's even grosser!" Sarah protests.

Karen laughs and looks out the window, her painful memory having moved on completely. As she watches the beach grass and scrub pines they are driving past, she once again says a little prayer to herself. "Thank you, God, for this family. Thank you, God, for these children and this husband. Thank you, God, for turning what was pain into joy. Thank you, God, for bringing me to this place today. Please help me to make the most out of every second of this life and not take one moment for granted."

"We need gas," Jack says.

"Oh, really?" Karen replies. "Well, let's be sure to get the best, most reliable, and excellent gas we can find."

Jack pauses. "Uh, gee, hon, I was just gonna stop at the Sunoco station. Did you have some special kind of gas in mind?"

"No, no. Sunoco would be just fine. I was just having a little daydream, that's all."

"About gas?" Jack asks incredulously.

"Fuel, honey. It was about fuel. Hey, I'll get out and pump."

Jack raises his eyebrows, not understanding what has transpired, but glad to accept the offer of Karen's help.

———

Some of the best moments in our lives are moments of connection. As humans, our most fulfilling moments center around deepening a connection or making progress in working toward a goal. The seemingly insignificant scene above shows what a major significance positive connection can hold. Loving connection can wipe out old pain and heal old wounds. Loving connection can provide the energy—the fuel, to use Karen's word—to overcome all kinds of adversity, as well as the inspiration to reach for lofty goals.

Connection need not always be explicitly stated or even felt two ways. Jack didn't have any idea what Karen was going through, yet Karen felt immensely connected to Jack and her family. We see this all the time in our connection with our young children. We feel more connected to them than perhaps any other beings alive, yet they can be furious with us as we feel such connection.

Between adults who know each other well and love each other deeply, the connection reverberates even in long periods of silence as they drive together, eat together, walk together, grow old together. As their connection deepens and grows, adults need fewer words, understand nonverbal cues, know each other's thoughts and feelings intuitively, and can dance together without moving a muscle. Such connection lies at the heart of the kind of ecstasy that can last a lifetime, if not forever.

Disconnection, on the other hand, lies at the heart of misery. When you feel disconnected from a person you love, a place you love, a group or cause you love, a pet you love, a hope you had, or a dream you cherished, this is the beginning of despair.

In a marriage, disconnection can slowly grow over time or erupt in a moment. People can grow apart without really knowing that it's happening until they wake up one morning and realize they're strangers, or they can imagine they are close only to discover some terrible secret that shatters connection in an instant.

We can't discuss all the causes of disconnection in this short book, but we can focus on one: distraction. Lack of attention. Minds that do not meet but go elsewhere.

This kind of disconnection can settle in slowly, disappointment by disappointment. It can look like this:

LUKE: They're giving me the salesperson-of-the-month award tonight.

TANYA: Oh.

LUKE: Can you come?

TANYA: It's my book group tonight.

LUKE: Oh.

TANYA: We're reading *To the Lighthouse*.

LUKE: Did you like it?

TANYA: I haven't read it, yet.

LUKE: Are you going to try to read it before you go?

TANYA: Maybe. But we usually talk more about our own lives at the group than about the book, so it really doesn't matter.

LUKE: Then why bother with having a book at all?

TANYA: (Pause) You really don't see why?

LUKE: Not really. If you don't read the books, why not just call it a social group? Why call it a book group?

TANYA: (Pause) You're sitting there and I'm sitting here.

LUKE: Yes, that's true.

TANYA: Why the funny look?

LUKE: I don't see how saying that I'm sitting here and you're sitting there answers my question. But it doesn't matter. I was just trying to make some conversation.

TANYA: Why? Has that ever helped?

LUKE: Helped what?

TANYA: You're sitting there and I'm sitting here. Don't you understand? We call it a book group because none of us wants to call it a desperate-women-in-search-of-meaningful-connection group. So we call it a book group. Makes it sound much more respectable. But after a few glasses of wine we truly don't care.

LUKE: I'm not getting you. Are you trying to be funny? That wouldn't be like you.

TANYA: No, it wouldn't, as far as you're concerned. But at the book group, I'm thought of as the funny one. I bet that surprises the living hell out of you.

LUKE: Living hell. Interesting turn of phrase.

TANYA: Oh, give me a break, Luke. Give me a break. What is it? Are you hurt because I don't want to give up my book group to come see you get your award tonight?

LUKE: No. I knew you wouldn't come. I'm hurt because this is all we do anymore.

TANYA: Anymore? It used to be different?

LUKE: Yes, it did. And you know it did.

TANYA: I do know it did. You have no idea how sad that makes me.

LUKE: So what do you want to do?

TANYA: I have my book group. I have my friends. I have my kids.

LUKE: *Our* kids.

TANYA: Technically, yes.

LUKE: What do you mean by that?

TANYA: What do you think I mean? Who is more the parent here?

LUKE: That is so unfair. I have to work. What would we do if I didn't bring in the money?

TANYA: That's your excuse.

LUKE: I can't believe how cruel you've become.

TANYA: And I can't believe how clueless you've become.

That's disconnection. Late stage. Not end stage yet, but getting there. Unless Luke and Tanya take some positive steps, they will be consigning themselves to the living hell they alluded to, which they now inhabit. Disconnection in a place, such as a marriage, that is supposed to be connected is one good description of living hell. Religious people talk about feeling disconnected from God as living hell. The secular version of that is feeling disconnected from the person you once loved, or wanted to love.

In the case of Luke and Tanya, we don't have enough information to know how they got to this spot. We only show it to you to caution you against it. Unfortunately, there are many ways to get to where they are. One of the major ways is simply to spend too much time not making enough time—for each other.

Then disconnection sets in like dry rot. You start to blame one another, and you spend the rest of your time together in conflict or avoidance. But this kind of disconnection, the disconnection that comes from lack of time together, is utterly preventable.

———

Disconnection is a modern epidemic. It is a terrible but unrecognized disease. It removes you from what matters most in your life and leaves you feeling depleted of vital juices.

Disconnection is an invisible vector, like a virus. Once it gets into your system, you feel sick. Like a vitamin deficiency, it causes a host of symptoms, without your understanding the underlying cause. You feel less energetic and ambitious than you usually are without knowing the reason, which only increases your stress and worry. You feel worse and worse, but you don't know why.

The why is disconnection. It's caused by a lack of what we call "the other vitamin C," or vitamin Connect.

Disconnection can kill you. It kills relationships all the time, but it can even take your life. How poignant and ironic it is that in our era of unprecedented electronic connection, people feel more and more interpersonally disconnected. Various academic authorities, such as political scientist Robert Putnam and social epidemiologist Lisa Berkman, both of Harvard, have documented this phenomenon in detail.

Yet, disconnection remains largely unrecognized and un-talked-about in general parlance. Not many patients come to us complaining of a severe case of "disconnection." They complain instead of fatigue, of low-level depression, of feeling crazy-busy, of having more to do than time to do it, and they complain that life is not what they want it to be.

In the case of a couple like Luke and Tanya, they would complain of drifting apart, of not feeling cared for by the other. They would complain of feeling disrespected and misunderstood by the other. They might even say they hate the other person, feel trapped, even suicidal. They would blame each other.

But, if the cause is the force of distraction, then the pieces can be put back together far more easily than if the cause is some deeper psychological issue.

Let's say the force of distraction is the cause. As we explain to Luke and Tanya that they have allowed themselves to become overstretched and overbooked, leading them to lose contact with each other, they at first protest and disagree, because they are in the *habit* of protesting and disagreeing. It's what they do. But then, one of them says maybe we have a point.

Then they protest that they had no choice but to obey the force of distraction. They protest they had too much to attend to. They backslide into blaming and saying it was the other person's fault. They were left with no choice. Our job then becomes with them, as it is in this book, to point out the many ways in which they *did, and do, in fact, have a choice.*

We help them to look at how they schedule their lives, how they allocate their time. The use of time—which we *do* have considerable control over, even if we *feel* as if we do not—provides an overlooked but practical and influential regulator of how a couple get along. With time goes mental and emotional energy, so the allocation of time means everything.

This is, or ought to be, a blame-free discussion. But it does carry huge emotional baggage. How a person spends his or her time is often more contentious in a couple than how a person spends money. When we work on this with couples, we simply inquire about daily schedules. We ask questions like:

- When do you get up?
- When do you have breakfast? With whom?
- When do you leave for work?
- When do you get home?
- How often do you go out together in the evening?
- How much time do you spend together, just the two of you, at home?
- How often do you make love?
- How much time do you spend with your kids?
- How much time do you spend with your friends?
- How much time do you spend pursuing a special hobby or activity you love?
- How much time do you spend relaxing?
- How much sleep do you get?
- How much physical exercise do you get?
- How much time do you spend in meditation or prayer?
- How much alone time do you have?
- How much together time do you have?
- How would each of you like to see the use of time change?

The last question, of course, invites conflict, but the previous questions have set the stage. If the couple can find new ways to spend more time together, then a deeper connection can develop. Without more time, it is not likely.

The thirty-day reconnection plan at the end of this book will give you thirty days' worth of ideas for reconnection. In the short term, try this: spend the first ten or fifteen minutes of every day in bed together just cuddling and talking. If you are both morning people, this will work well for you. If you are night people, try it before you both go to sleep. If one of you likes morning and the other likes evening, then try finding another time in the day that works for you, if not to cuddle, then just to be together and to chat.

The key here is to use the tool of time in your favor, as opposed to using it to your detriment, which is what many couples unwittingly do.

The time is there. The trick is to use it to your advantage.

Two simple tools—time and attention—combine to create empathy, which can lead into the magnificent, transformative world of intimate connection.

FIVE

Distracters and Organizers

In our world of input overload, some people naturally do better than others at keeping on track and staying focused. Some people are innately more talented in this way than other people. It has to do with their wiring, not their character, level of effort, or essential goodness. A great mistake many couples make is to treat the issue as if it were about goodness and effort rather than neurological differences. They make a "moral diagnosis" instead of a biological one.

Most people do not appreciate the genetic, biological aspect of the capacity to pay attention. Most people attribute paying attention *entirely* to effort. If you *want* to attend, the assumption goes, you can and will. Therefore a spouse will blame his or her mate for spacing out, when in fact blame is not warranted—and is quite counterproductive. In this chapter we introduce a more accurate, and far more useful, way of understanding attention and organization than the moral model, which explains everything in terms of goodness, character, and effort.

While the modern forces of distraction pull both members of a couple away from each other, usually one member is more susceptible to these forces than the other, and one member is better able to resist them, as well as better able to engage in conversation and to organize life.

For the purposes of this book, we wanted to make up a term to distinguish the better organizer from the less skilled. We settled on a simple shorthand. We call the more distracted member of the couple D, for distracted or distracter, and the more organized we call O, for organized or organizer. These traits are not permanently set, as people can switch roles in different contexts, at times one person being the O and at other times the D.

In addition, sometimes the person who is usually the D can feel as if she is married to distraction, while the person who is usually the O can look to her mate to do the organizing. The roles can switch back and forth, each person stepping in to help, or stepping out, according to the host of forces that lead us to do what we do. The shorthand D and O serve not as fixed roles but roles that are usually in flux. The shorthand is useful, however, to describe conflicts that arise when the roles become unbalanced or in conflict.

Two D's can marry one another (leading to happy chaos or a disaster!), or two O's can marry one another (leading to blissful order or organized boredom). In some marriages, the traits of the D and the O are fairly evenly divided between the two members.

Here are more examples of how these roles play out in a relationship: D tends to lose track of what's being talked about in a conversation, as his or her eyes wander to some random person walking by or to a television or other screen within eyeshot or just off into space. D tends to disappear when it is time to go somewhere. D tends to make plans but then not follow through and complete them. D tends to be difficult to engage in conversation. D has trouble being on time or making deadlines. D has trouble paying bills on time, managing money, keeping track of details, cleaning up, and in general getting done the boring tasks that need to get done. D is also moodier and less consistent.

But D also tends to provide the spark, the energy, the fun. D is more spontaneous, more spirited, more creative, more inventive. D is the idea person—but often lacks the follow-through. In its most extreme form, D has actual attention deficit disorder, or ADD. But, as we've stated, this is a small percentage of the adult population, about 5 percent. On the other hand, the number of adults who have many D traits is anything but small. Modern life is so distracting that it *creates* D's.

O is the reverse. O makes the trains run on time. O makes the doctor's appointments, the vet appointments, the parent-teacher meeting appointments, and the host of other essential appointments. O sees to it that the lights get turned out and the doors get locked before everyone has gone to bed, and O sees to it that all who need to get up in fact do get up on time. O pays the bills (or ought to pay the bills—sometimes D insists on doing it and makes a mess of it). O initiates conversations, tries to keep people engaged in conversation before they turn to the TV, works hard to keep up lines of communication within the family and the community, and in general carries the larger portion of the burden of organizing. O is the more emotionally steady. O is also more aware of the feelings of others, even though D can be extraordinarily intuitive and empathic when he or she is paying attention.

O is the more inhibited, the more linear, the less intuitive. O works hard to make things right, so hard that O can carry a fair amount of resentment that he/she has to do so much of this work.

Of course, some O and some D is in each member of every couple. But in today's world, with its higher-than-ever levels of distraction and demands, one member of most couples tends to emerge more the D, and one more the O.

The tendency to be a D or an O is innate, inborn, genetically transmitted, and hardwired. It has little to do with effort, character, willpower, goodness, or any of the other "moral diagnoses" people invoke to blame each other for being who they can't help but be.

Other ways to describe D and O would be as follows:

O is the finder; D is the one who loses things.
O takes on a parental role in the relationship; D is the child.
O is aware of what's going on with other people; D tends to be engrossed in whatever he/she is doing.
O feels burdened; D feels guilty.

O is the nagger; D is the nagged.

O seems the more responsible; D seems the less responsible.

O does more than his/her share of the undesirable work; D does less but often is unaware that he/she is doing less.

O often feels at the end of his/her rope as to how to get through to D; D feels as if he/she is always about to be chastised for something.

O wants to talk about it, whatever "it" is; D wants to get away.

O has trouble keeping up his/her sense of humor; D wishes O would lighten up.

O favors caution; D likes risk.

O wants to make a plan to make things better; D hates plans.

O is open to psychotherapy; D would rather have a root canal than see a therapist.

O is a realist; D is a dreamer.

O resents the role of being the organizer but can't let go of it for fear everything would fall apart; D is unaware of how close things can come to falling apart.

O gets tired of being the "heavy," but feels he/she has to be or things would fall apart; D gets tired of being told what to do by O.

O remembers; D forgets.

O gets stuck in anger; D gets stuck in shame.

O feels D just doesn't get it; D feels O is too touchy and controlling.

O craves an end to the struggle; so does D.

As we explain these roles to people, they often say, "Why don't you just come out and say it? O is the woman and D is the man." While that is sometimes the case, it is far from always the case. Many times the man will be more the O and the woman will be more the D.

Furthermore, the O and D roles can alternate, as stated before, depending on the context and the situation. For example, D might become O while organizing the kids to go to a soccer practice, or O might become D while at a nightclub or while taking a walk.

While being an O or a D is an innate tendency, it is also dependent on context. A certain situation can bring out a person's D side, while another situation can bring out his/her O side. For example, a person might be an utter O while reading a map, but a complete D when in a museum.

Again, we need to debunk the role of willpower because often spouses will blame each other for being who they are in a given context. One might say, "Why can you be so laser-beam focused when you're reading a map but such a total space shot when we went to the Museum of Fine Arts last Sunday? You just refuse to get into the museum experience!" But chances are good it was not a matter of refusal but innate predisposition.

Not only do differing situations bring out the inborn O or D tendencies, no O and no D fits every single one of the descriptions of O and D listed above. Indeed, they may fit only a few. The descriptions are intended to give a feel for the different roles. In most couples, each member will have some O and some D. The boundaries between the two blur.

In fact, there may be no D and no O in the couple, just two amalgams of both. Though these couples do not take on the D and O roles, they still contend with the many forces of distraction and overload that we discuss in this book. They will find the O and D concepts useful in describing themselves to each other and avoiding the struggles caused by the moral-diagnosis model.

We describe the O and D roles individually because, over time, one member of the couple commonly takes on a bit more O than D and vice versa. Once you see this, and you understand the O and D concepts, it becomes easier to talk about what's going on without getting into an argument over it and slipping into the I'm-good-and-you're-bad mode.

Remember, these roles are involuntary. D does not *choose* to be distracted, nor does O *choose* to be the more focused. Genes determine the roles, as do early training in life, inborn temperament and predilections, and other unconscious or involuntary forces.

D does not say, "Gee, I think I'll be messy," or, "Gee, I think I'll be hard to reach emotionally, because I know that drives my spouse crazy and I love to see him/her suffer." And O does not say, "I really love the role of organizer, it makes me feel so powerful and in control so that I can lord it over my spouse," or, "Wow, hounding my spouse is such fun! How did I ever live without someone to hound?"

Put like that, you can see how ridiculous it sounds to see these roles as voluntary, but still most people see them exactly as that: conscious and deliberate choices made out of laziness or to defy and frustrate the other person.

But stop and think about it. Not many people want to spend their entire marriage fighting with their mate. Few people *enjoy* upsetting their spouse. Not many people like getting into trouble with their partner or spending hours in stony silence. Most people who live together want to get along. They desire harmony and laughter. They want to mesh, not strip each other's gears.

Another word of caution. Most people have a bit of the psychologist in them. Sometimes people resort to popular psychological explanations to explain why their partner is so difficult. They end up using psychological diagnoses as weapons. "You're so passive-aggressive!" one will bark at the other.

"You're nothing but a selfish narcissist!" another will say.

"You're impossible to live with, you're so OCD," another will scream. "It's like being married to Detective Monk!"

For the purposes of this book, we caution you against using certain psychological concepts that have drifted into popular culture. They are useful concepts in some contexts, but they can mislead, distort, and in general *add* to conflict rather than help resolve it.

1. The passive-aggressive personality. Most people recognize this as someone who can't disagree directly and so expresses aggression passively. For example, the passive-aggressive individual might agree to take out the trash, then walk blithely right past it without moving it one inch. Instead of saying, "No, I won't take out the trash," he/she expresses refusal passively, i.e., by not doing it.

It is tempting to dub D as passive-aggressive because he/she so often agrees to do something, then doesn't do it. The assumption is that D chooses not to take out the trash. Instead of refusing straight out, he/she passively avoids the task.

But all the term *passive-aggressive* does in this context is fuel argument. It becomes a fancy, psychobabble way of calling D a jerk. Instead of saying, "You jerk!" you say, "Stop being so passive-aggressive," and you're launched off into a fight.

While D might be passive-aggressive, it is more likely that, being D, he/she easily forgets, easily gets distracted, easily finds some other focus for attention. This is not voluntary.

It is much more helpful if O, understanding this, can laugh and say, "You're amazing, D. I could never say I'm going to take out the trash and then walk right past it. We are so different."

O understands that D can actually forget to do something immediately after agreeing to do it. Like the absentminded professor, he/she has his mind elsewhere, not because he/she wants to be difficult, but, simply, because that is how he/she is wired.

Of course, you do not want D to use his/her being D as an excuse. But it is a powerful and useful explanation, far more useful than the label *passive-aggressive*.

Handling the situation this way, you're not overlooking that the trash needs to be taken out, nor are you taking it out yourself, but in a humorous, nonthreatening fashion you are raising an issue to discuss.

Before you invoke the concept of passive-aggressive and the arguments it so easily leads to, first consider the role of D as being hardwired, not a character flaw.

2. The obsessive-compulsive personality. Obsessive-compulsive disorder (OCD) and its milder cousin, the obsessive-compulsive personality, have entered into common parlance thanks in part to movies such as *As Good as It Gets* and TV shows such as *Monk*. The hallmarks of the obsessive-compulsive personality do not include the rituals and superstitions that those shows have made famous, but do include many tendencies that the person in the O role might exhibit.

These include a tendency to want to be in control; a need for order, cleanliness, and structure; more than ordinary discomfort with chaos or disorganization; a tendency to feel competitive even when the situation does not warrant it; and carrying built-up anger that can explode without warning.

But before you start calling your O spouse obsessive-compulsive and telling him/her to get into therapy, consider to what extent the situation you're living in cries out for someone to take charge and get things organized and how trying to do so without help could stir up anger in anyone.

Once again, the term *obsessive-compulsive* can become just a smart-sounding stand-in term for *jerk*. So, when your O spouse says to you, "I really wish you would clean up the toolshed this weekend and take care of that pile of junk in the backyard," instead of snapping back, "Oh, you are so OCD, control, control, control, and any little thing out of place just sets you off," try using this alternative: "I could ignore the toolshed and that pile of junk for years because just about anything seems more interesting to me, but you absolutely *can't* ignore them. The mess drives you nuts. It's interesting how different we are. What you're asking isn't unreasonable. If I put it at the top of my list, will you help me not get sidetracked and remind me? I promise not to call you a nag if you do."

This way, instead of cudgeling O with a psych term, you are seeing the problem from his/her point of view and acknowledging both the reasonableness of it and your tendency to ignore or avoid the task. By asking him/her to remind you, you instantly turn a potential nagger into a helper and a potential argument into an opportunity for collaboration and growth.

3. The narcissistic personality. This is probably the most overused and misunderstood of all the concepts imported from psychiatry into common discourse. Freud's definition of *narcissism*, "the libidinal cathexis of the self," makes *no* sense to anyone outside the profession, and the current textbook definition of *narcissism* is far more elaborate than most people realize.

Most people (including many professionals who should know better) use *narcissism* as a fancy put-down, a dis, a big word that means "selfish." In fact, there aren't that many true narcissists, thank goodness, as these people are locked in an emotional prison, unable to give or receive love. However, just about all of us can seem selfish now and then. We devote the next chapter to discussing this concept and how it can be dangerously misunderstood.

The real culprits in the D and O conflict are not some psychiatric diagnoses but the enormous organizational demands of modern life, the vast number of obligations and opportunities we each face every day, the alluring and ubiquitous forces of distraction that surround us, and the speed at which we are all expected to deal with what's coming at us.

The D and O roles have emerged more clearly in couples these days because the forces that create them are more powerful than ever. The roles do not represent conscious choices, but natural tendencies.

It is crucial to understand the involuntary nature of these roles because until you do understand it, you will tend to blame the other person for not being the way you want him/her to be. You will tend to take personally the other's tendencies and believe that everything could change for the better if only the other person would try harder.

While trying harder helps just about any problem, this problem will not yield to effort alone. You can't *overpower* the problem. You need to understand it. You need to see the other person not as your adversary or as a slacker but as a person whose natural inclinations and modus operandi in life differ from yours.

It is not *better* to be an O than a D or vice versa. But for the two to get along in any close relationship, it is best to begin by understanding the other person's natural way, be it O or D. Then you can start to create a plan that will actually work.

For example, in our marriage, I, Ned, am usually the D, and Sue is the O. I say "usually" because, as often happens, in some situations, such as in airports or in dealing with telemarketers, I am more the O. But most of the time, Sue is the organizer. She pays the bills. She makes the schedules for the kids. She remembers when one of us needs to go to the pet store to buy more dog food. She sets up our dinner parties.

I, on the other hand, come up with more of the ideas for fun times. I provide more of the humor and energy for spur-of-the-moment let's-do-it outings. I am more likely to be the one who takes a risk. The roles do overlap. Sue can also take a risk. And I can change lightbulbs.

The point is that we have worked out a resentment-free way (most of the time!) of understanding and dealing with each other's innate tendencies. Neither of us feels superior to the other. We value the talents one has that the other lacks, which allows us to support each other (most of the time) rather than criticize or struggle.

It's not that we never criticize or argue. We do. We are both stubborn. We can argue over the most ridiculous, petty things. Usually the subtext is a power struggle. Such is marriage. But we have worked out a way between us to get along quite well most of the time. Understanding the concepts of D and O has helped us to do this.

SIX

Seemingly Selfish

In the context of being married to distraction, O may be tempted to call D selfish or a narcissist because D seems so wrapped up in his/her own world. D seems unaware or uncaring of the needs of others. D seems to care only about his/her own desires. So, O is tempted to hurl the epithet *narcissist* at D. "You're nothing but a selfish narcissist!" That'll fix him!

Of course, as with tossing around the terms *passive-aggressive* and *OCD*, all the epithet does is make matters worse. It allows O to overlook that D is not being this way on purpose, and it attributes serious character pathology (being an actual narcissist is a bad problem indeed) where there is actually none. But calling people names can cause problems in its own right.

So, instead of calling D a narcissist, try this instead: "You know, when I speak to you and you don't respond, I get so frustrated and angry that I want to start calling you names. Can you suggest to me what I should do instead?"

Selfishness seems so on the rise in the past decade for a reason. As the "inputs" of life mount and organizational demands reach crazy levels, most people lose some or much of their capacity to attend to others. In couples this often gets misinterpreted as a character flaw. In frustration, the member of the couple who feels neglected calls the other member selfish. This is not meant as a helpful hint but as an insult, a cudgel used to punish, not enlighten.

This is yet another trap that the moral model sets for couples. So successfully does the moral model indoctrinate us that we are ever eager to pounce when we see what we take to be a character flaw. Gotcha! Empathy disappears. The effort to understand ceases. The attack begins.

One of the most common "flaws" one member of a couple detects in the other is selfishness. "He just doesn't know how to think about anyone except himself." "She is far more concerned about going shopping than trying to understand the stress I'm under at work." "It's just not in his repertoire to think of me unless I wave my hands up and down." "She cares about her career first, her weight second, and everything else a distant third."

Selfish is one of those words that are often used to beat up someone else when you're not getting what you want. Sure, a person may be extremely self-centered, seemingly even to the point of being a narcissist, but, as we stated in the previous chapter, true narcissists are much rarer than they seem.

At first glance, modern life seems to teem with narcissists. Self-centeredness seems to abound. Nowhere is this more a problem than in the world of intimate relationships. Closeness—a truly connected and shared life—is hard to come by. What's going on? Have we seen a sudden upsurge in narcissism and self-centeredness? Have years of affluence and materialism eroded people's commitment to others and replaced it with a commitment to the self?

The answer—we think—is not so much that we have grown selfish but that we have become too busy for our own good. Much of the apparent selfishness, even the seeming narcissism, may be more a function of crazy-busy modern life than of character defects or a decline in goodness. The way we live may be inducing an inadvertent epidemic of seeming selfishness and what looks like narcissism.

True narcissism is just not as common as it seems these days. In case the term is not familiar to you, here is a quick sketch of a narcissist. The truly narcissistic person is unable to give or receive love. He (although it may be she) craves attention and needs praise to fill a gaping inner abyss. The narcissist feels empty and disconnected. He carries with him no images of people he felt or feels loved by, nor does he carry images of people he loved or loves. Lacking what psychiatrists call positive introjects—images of people who loved him, and images of himself as a lovable and loving person—he must live a life devoid of what sustains most of us. He is desperate, dangerously low on self-esteem, confidence, and a sense of basic security.

But he hides his vulnerabilities because they fill him with shame. Instead, he tries to appear better than everyone else. He fashions a false self to put on, like a fancy, tailored suit. He wears this accomplished, confident false self to impress the world and assuage his painful inner feelings of hatred of himself, hatred of others, and hatred of life.

He is a walking cauldron of rage at all those people who have not given him what he wants: love, admiration, power, prestige. He can usually keep a lid on his rage because he knows it will cost him the admiration he so desperately seeks, but now and then, when he feels slighted, he explodes.

He often develops phenomenal skills and proficiencies in the world, not in order to contribute to the world or for the joy of developing a skill, but to extract from the world as much praise and attention as he possibly can. He seeks to become a star to make up for how thoroughly unstarlike he actually feels. He is ruthless and cruel in his pursuit of stardom because stardom means life or death to him. He needs constant adulation because he dies inside without it.

The narcissist is deft in offering praise to carefully selected others in order to manipulate them to love him, but he means none of it. Indeed, he hates those he praises because he resents having to curry their favor. He feels the world should come to him, and he detests the world for not doing so. When the world does not come to him, as it tends not to do, he mounts his attack. He plots and schemes his way to the top. He is artful in moving others out of his way in order to take center stage. He is also notoriously vicious when he feels even the mildest slight. He will attack the person he sensed slighted him with a ferocity far out of proportion to what the imagined slight deserved. He takes delight in reducing others in their own eyes, as his kind of misery loves company. But no matter how much adulation and praise he garners, it never fills the void inside; his void is a bottomless pit. The person who falls in love with a narcissist—and, tragically, many people do because they are so charming—is doomed to a life of loneliness and emotional isolation for as long as the relationship lasts. Unfortunately, the narcissist is often able to devise ways to make the relationship last, using charisma, seduction, money, and power to control his mate.

As you can see from that description, true narcissism is not common. It takes time to become that impaired. It takes an unusual set of circumstances, a love-deprived childhood, a selfish set of parents or other non-caregivers, to produce a narcissist. True narcissism is one of the worst outcomes of a disconnected childhood. It's rare, thank goodness.

On the other hand, what is not rare these days is the *semblance* of narcissism. Many people seem so preoccupied with their own projects and problems and so invested in getting ahead that they can seem not to care for others. They can seem unable to love. They can seem to be in love only with themselves and their chances for gain and glory.

Today's world is creating pseudonarcissists, people who seem utterly self-involved but actually are not. Rather than self-involved, the pseudonarcissist is overwhelmed. Being overwhelmed, he is unable to give enough attention to others to create rewarding relationships.

Not only people in marriages but also those in close friendships can feel rejected or not cared for. These people complain of the selfishness of the friend or the mate. They feel angry at the other for being too wrapped up in his own world to pay attention to them. But as you look more closely, what you often find is that the supposedly selfish person is not selfish but rather stressed, worried, preoccupied with real problems, and crazy busy. Due to these pressures, he loses his ability to attend to the needs of the people closest to him. He regrets being emotionally unavailable as much as anyone else.

The good news is that pseudonarcissism can be fixed in a relatively short time, if a person is willing to make some concrete changes. True narcissism, on the other hand, takes as many years to cure as it took to create, and even then there is slim hope of a good result.

The pseudonarcissist is the overwhelmed person we can all identify with at times. Overload has led him to appear to be self-centered, uncaring about the needs of others, while, in fact, he simply does not have neurons free and available to devote to what's going on in the lives of others. That may sound like selfishness or narcissism, but isn't. It's overload.

This should provide solid hope for the women or men who think they're married to a hopelessly selfish or narcissistic person. Before you reach that conclusion and head for the divorce attorney, consider this other possibility.

Consider that he might be juggling too much. Consider that she might seem as if she has blinders on because she had to develop the blinders to deal with overload. Consider that he might not be the selfish bastard you think he is but rather an overtaxed man who can't regulate his own life. Consider that she might not be the selfish diva you think she's become but a stressed-out woman in need of some love— but can't even find time to ask for it.

Looked at this way, the selfish narcissist may rather be a frustrated D in need of some O. The therapy could go like this:

SALLY: When you come home, you walk right past me as if I didn't exist. I could be standing there stark naked or hanging by a noose from the ceiling and you wouldn't see me.

PAUL: So you've told me many times.

THERAPIST: What's your explanation, Sally?

SALLY: I think he is simply a selfish man. He doesn't know how to notice others. I'm not surprised, though. You should meet his parents.

PAUL: I am not like my parents.

THERAPIST: What's your explanation, Paul?

PAUL: Honestly, I'm tired when I get home. I know that sounds stupid, but I am worn-out and beat-up by the end of my day.

SALLY: Don't you think I'm tired, too? But I am able to notice the kids, feed the dog, pick up the messes, get dinner ready, and greet you with a smile.

PAUL: Let's not compete over who's the most tired.

THERAPIST: It's fair to say you're both tired. When people are tired, it's hard to notice what's going on.

SALLY: I do it. Why can't he?

PAUL: I think I do do it. At least I try to do it.

SALLY: That's just my point. You try but you can't. You're just a hopelessly self-centered person.

THERAPIST: You might be right, Sally, but before we go there, how about if we consider a much simpler and easier-to-fix diagnosis. How about if we consider the possibility that Paul is just not as good at juggling all that has to be done and managing stress as you are? How about if we consider the possibility that Paul is more of a distracted kind of person and you are more of a focused and organized kind of person?

SALLY: Well, that much is true for sure.

PAUL: Yes, it is true.

SALLY: But so what? Where does that get us?

THERAPIST: Well, for one thing, that gets us out of the moral model, the model that condemns Paul for being selfish, and as we all learned as kids, selfish is bad. Paul being less organized than you, Sally, may be annoying, but it isn't morally reprehensible.

SALLY: But still, what do we do with that?

THERAPIST: I think part of what makes it hard for Paul to notice you and give his attention to you is that in some ways he agrees with you, that he is bad for being who he is, and he doesn't know what to do about it. This leads him to avoid you somewhat because he feels such intense disapproval from you. But if we shift the model from a moral one to a more mundane but fixable one of distraction versus organization, then Paul might feel less guilty and condemned, regain some enthusiasm, and be better able to change.

PAUL: I actually think he's right, honey.

SALLY: How do I know this isn't another excuse, another cop-out?

THERAPIST: You're right to be skeptical, Sally. You've been burned. You've gotten your hopes up in the past only to have them dashed. It's understandable why you're angry and why you're skeptical. But you wouldn't be here if you didn't want things to change for the better.

SALLY: I do. I really do want things to change for the better. I just don't want to get my hopes up and see them dashed again.

PAUL: I know you have a hard time believing me because I promise to do better and then I don't come through, but I do think part of the problem is that I have become afraid of letting you down and so I don't ask you for help when I need it, and I don't tell you when I'm having trouble because I don't want to disappoint you.

SALLY: But, Paul, if we can't communicate honestly with each other, we'll never get anywhere.

PAUL: I know. That's why this seems like a kind of breakthrough maybe. If I can just tell you what I'm up against without worrying that you're going to disapprove . . .

SALLY: Now I feel like the bad guy again.

PAUL: No, the bad guy is our lack of communication. We both play a part in it.

SALLY: Yes, you're right. I don't mean to be so angry so often. It's just that I get tired, too.

PAUL: Believe me, I understand that.

From that point, the therapist can begin to work with Paul and Sally in concrete terms on how to help Paul juggle better, de-stress better, and notice Sally better, while helping Sally to use her considerable skills not to punish Paul but to help him become more adept in managing modern life. In return, Paul can begin to grow closer to Sally, offer his love to her in the ways he once did, rediscover the fun he used to bring to the relationship, and make the music that he used to make.

Replacing the moral, blame-and-shame model with a model that emphasizes empathy, curiosity, and problem solving can give a couple a fresh start.

SEVEN

The Big Struggle

The art of being wise is the art of knowing what to overlook.

—WILLIAM JAMES

Judgment easily becomes the enemy of understanding. It can create a pattern of attack and defend, defend and attack, leading to ongoing struggle.

The struggles can seem endless, pointless, agonizingly destructive, and, worst of all, unstoppable.

A hallmark, unfortunately, of being married to distraction is struggle. Arguing, fighting, complaining, nagging, quarreling, disagreeing. It is no way to live. But struggle is the inevitable consequence of the various obstacles we've discussed: the force of distraction, overload, cracked conversations, the soufflé effect, lack of attention, and all the rest. When the struggle becomes severe, as it often does, we simply call it "the big struggle." It can dominate your relationship to the point that it seems you are only intimate when you are fighting, a sadomasochistic pattern that Edward Albee made famous in his play *Who's Afraid of Virginia Woolf?*

It can ignite without your being aware of any conflict to start with. It's common in busy couples for ordinary conversation suddenly to lurch into struggle, like this:

"Bye, honey. Love you."

"Love you, too."

"Don't forget the lawn guy needs to get paid."

"Okay. Good luck with the school people today.... What do you mean the lawn guy needs to get paid? You said you'd do that."

"No, you said you'd do that. I don't have the money set aside for it."

"Well, damn it, you ought to. You do this all the time. How are we ever going to save money if you're spending every extra cent we have? You don't even have the small change in your account to pay the lawn guy? This makes me crazy."

"Well, you make me crazy. All you ever do is attack me."

"Me attack you? What am I supposed to do when all you do is screw up?"

"I didn't screw up the deal with the lawn guy. You did. You said you'd pay him."

"I did not. I will not take responsibility for something I didn't do, I don't care how loud you yell."

"I am not yelling. That's your habit, not mine."

And on it goes.

It's a struggle you don't want, a struggle you don't feel you created, a struggle that wasn't there when you got together in the first place, a struggle that seems simultaneously petty and profound, and a struggle that both parties yearn to escape from but just can't figure out how.

It's petty because you're arguing over what seems like stupid stuff—who's going to pay the lawn guy—yet it's profound because this struggle is always rising up when you're together.

It becomes like a dance. Attack and defend. Defend and attack. Welcome to the big struggle.

It is a struggle of varying dimensions. It is a struggle to get the other person's attention, or a struggle to justify why providing that attention is so difficult; it's a struggle to make time for each other; a struggle to get done all that has to get done; a struggle to divide chores and other work fairly and evenly; a struggle to bring the other person into a way of relating that is fulfilling to both of you; a struggle to be heard and to hear; a struggle to get your way or to compromise gracefully; a struggle to prioritize and get done what matters most. Forces of distraction intensify all these struggles and add to the force of other struggles as well. Increasingly, couples who are married to distraction live their lives feeling as if they were driving on square wheels. It takes a ton of effort to go just a few hundred yards, and those few hundred yards dish out many bumps. Sometimes you think it just isn't worth it.

Until you are aware of what's going on, the roles of D and O usually intensify these struggles into the big struggle, an exaggeration of the ordinary struggles inherent in any intimate relationship. Once your honeymoon is over, all couples, married to distraction or not, get into various kinds of struggles. If you have done this, don't worry. Rare is the couple who hasn't. But when the roles of D and O become accentuated and not understood, ordinary struggles can morph into the big struggle.

Of course, some struggle is inevitable in all marriages or live-in relationships. Look at all the choices a couple have to make, some big, some small, but all choices that require a decision. Some of the choices can be made individually, but still lead to resentment if the other member of the couple does not approve or agree, while other choices must be made together as a couple. Examples of both kinds of choices include:

- What temperature do we want the bedroom at night or the house/apartment during the day?
- Whom are you going to vote for in the election?
- What shall we have for dinner tonight?
- What shall we watch on TV?
- How much TV and other electronics shall we allow the children?
- How do we discipline our children?
- Who does the laundry?
- Who cooks? Who cleans up?

- Into what account or accounts does the money that each of us earns go?
- Who decides what we can afford and what we buy?
- If one wants to make love and the other doesn't, what happens?
- Who is the better driver?

The list could go on for dozens of pages. The point here is to remind you what an obvious setup for a struggle marriage, or any close, live-in relationship, creates. Unless one of you is utterly passive or submissive, struggles will inevitably arise.

The D and O roles are a prime source of struggle. If you can understand what's going on in terms of D and O, rather than in terms of good and bad or right and wrong, you can often avoid the pain of the big struggle and get to some sort of harmony.

Let us give you an example of how quickly D and O can lock horns. Let's say in this case Ellen, the wife, is the O, and Mark, the husband, is the D. Let's say Ellen has cooked dinner for Mark and their three kids, and dinner has just ended. Mark gets up from the table and goes into the den, where he turns on a baseball game. The kids clear their plates and the rest of the table, as is their routine, and they go off to their rooms to play or study, depending on their age.

Ellen sits at the table clenching her fists. Mark has no clue that she is seething. A few minutes pass, then Mark hears Ellen making more than the usual amount of noise as she does the dishes. He doesn't hear anything break, but he hears such clanging of pots and slamming of cupboard doors that he knows something is wrong. He gets up and goes into the kitchen.

"Ellen, what's wrong?"

Ellen wheels around, a spatula in her hand, and says, "What's wrong? That's what's wrong! Your asking me what's wrong is what's wrong. You don't even remember that just two days ago we had a conversation about how much work around the house I am left with having to do, and you don't even remember that in that conversation you said to me from now on, every night, before you got up from the dinner table, you would ask me what you could do to help me, whether it was with the dishes or the kids or whatever. You don't even remember that I started to cry, I was so happy. You don't even remember that I told you that it was the evenings that were hardest on me, and that it would mean so much to me if I could feel that we were working as a team, and you don't even remember that you said, sure, that was the least you could do. I was so happy. I was on cloud nine. Then, when it didn't happen last night, I said to myself, don't nag, he probably has some reason, but then tonight, when you just got up, as if we never, ever, had that conversation, well, I wanted to scream, I wanted to throw something at you. But, of course, I didn't. I waited until I had some measure of control, and then I did the dishes. Loudly. Does any of this jog your memory?"

Mark has been standing there, listening, remembering the conversation, feeling ashamed. But he doesn't like to feel ashamed. Something snaps inside him and he suddenly takes the offensive. Defend and attack. Attack and defend. "Ellen, I am so tired of you and your endless complaints. There's always something I haven't done right. It's never 'Gee, Mark, thanks for going out and busting your hump every day to support this family.' No, it's never that. It's always, always about what I *haven't* done. Well, I'm tired of it."

Tears are now streaming down Ellen's face. "*You're* tired of it? Do you know how tired of it *I* am? Do you have even the remotest idea of what it's like to be me? No, you don't. And you never will."

———

We can interrupt the scene now. You can imagine how it will play out. They will continue to struggle and to fight, their remarks will get progressively more nasty and personal, they will make threats, they will say things they will later regret, they will hurt each other emotionally, maybe even physically. If they are lucky, the kids won't hear—but kids usually do hear.

They will go to bed hurt and angry. Maybe in the same bed, maybe not.

They love each other in their way, and they love their children, so they will not separate or divorce. They might go into couples therapy, which might or might not help. The most likely outcome is that they will struggle onward, less happy than they ought to be, less happy than they deserve to be, and less happy than their kids need them to be.

And on, and on, they struggle on. Heroic, often; persistent, usually; wishing for a better way, always.

We wouldn't be writing this book if we didn't know that there is a better way. There is a better way than wistful resignation. There is a better way, for sure, than ongoing struggle.

———

Let's look back at Ellen and Mark and show how things could have gone differently.

At the end of dinner, Mark goes into the den to watch TV. He has forgotten the conversation he had with Ellen two days prior. He is a D. Ellen, aware of Mark being a D, doesn't take it personally. She gets up, goes into the den, and asks Mark, "Remember the conversation we had two days ago about how you were going to help?"

Curtailing a struggle begins with empathy. Sue often suggests to couples that they imagine they are sitting next to one another on top of a mountain. "Now look down," Sue says, "and tell each other what you see." Each will see a different view. Same mountain, same vantage point, different descriptions of what each sees. This is obvious but worth stating because couples often forget how different their views are. Sue reminds them that just as what they see from the mountaintop differs, the reality one of them is living in is not at all the reality that the other is living in.

For people to get along intimately they must understand this jarring fact of life: we are separate individuals even if we love each other and live together. Obviously, it's good to know something about the reality your partner is living in instead of just assuming she/he lives in the same reality as you. Yet, unless we stop and think, we can easily fall into the trap of assuming our realities match.

Few couples ever sit down and listen closely to the other describe his or her view from the mountaintop. The conversation could begin with these questions:

1. As you look out at your life, what do you see?
2. As you look at yourself, what do you see?
3. As you look at me, what do you see?
4. As you look at us together, what do you see?

This is not a short conversation. You cannot wrap it up in one sitting. Really, this conversation ought to go on for the duration of your lives together.

In this first phase, this phase of trying to work toward a better way than the way of struggle, you can carry on this conversation in two or three sittings. Give yourselves an hour or so each time.

An hour? Who has an hour? That's just the point. *To bring about change, you have to make time for one another.* If you are married to distraction, if you are struggling more than is good for you, if you love your partner but you want a happier marriage or relationship, you must, first of all, commit to change, and to do that you must clear out some time for each other.

You may also feel awkward. You may find it almost laughable. "My spouse and I sit down and systematically ask these serious questions?" you might ask. "Not gonna happen! We'd start, and then one of us would laugh, or one of us would get annoyed, or we'd get just plain bored. It's all just too self-helpy. Maybe it sounds good on paper, but in real life, that's just not how the two of us interact. It's not realistic."

So, make it realistic. Figure out a way to have these conversations that allows you to be yourselves. Use the four questions above as a guide. You could even begin by making fun of the questions. For example: "Okay, so we're supposed to look out at our lives and see what we see. I see a big mess. What do you see, honey?"

"Yeah, a big mess sums it up pretty well."

"Next question. As you look at yourself, what do you see? Well, as I look at me, I see a middle-aged man who's working his butt off to keep things afloat and can't seem to find the time to have much fun. What do you see when you look at yourself, honey? Gee, isn't doing this fun?"

"Yes, wow, haven't had this much fun since my root canal. What do I see when I look at myself? A middle-aged woman who's trying her best to make the most out of what she has. I never became the pediatrician I wanted to become, I became a mom instead and got over-involved with the school to make up for my lack of a career. I see me becoming more and more like my own mother, which scares the living daylights out of me. Next question?"

"What do you see when you look at me?"

"I see a man who doesn't know how good he is. I see a man I worry about because he works too hard. I see the love of my life and I worry he isn't happy. What do you see when you look at me?"

"I see a woman who is trying to do too much. I see a woman who is not happy but is doing her best not to complain about it. I look at you and I feel guilty that I can't make you happy."

"It's not up to you to make me happy."

"It's up to us both to try, though, don't you think?"

Pretty soon, in spite of yourselves, you'll be having the kind of conversation you need to have to bring about change.

We offer this sample dialogue just to show that it doesn't have to be phony, self-helpy, and pat. You can have this conversation with your spouse and still be real. You can laugh, poke fun, and still get at some important truths about each other and your lives together.

If you do not have the time to do this exercise together now, we include it in the workbook at the end of the book. If you "work the workbook," you will have time set aside to ask these questions of each other as part of that experience.

Developing empathy, true empathy, is the most important step you can take toward ending a struggle and finding a better way. Instead of just telling your partner your complaints, you must first of all discover what life is like from the point of view of your partner.

It is possible to feel empathy—true understanding of the other person's reality—but also to feel anger. For example, you can genuinely empathize and understand what led your husband to have an affair, but you can feel angry nonetheless. We do not mean to imply that empathy cancels out anger or any other hostile feeling. Rather, meaningful progress in resolving differences must include a genuine empathic understanding of the other person.

Most people talk a good game along these lines, but they do not mean it. They say they want to understand the other person, but they do not take the time and do the work. They don't even know what it means to understand another person. It is an alien skill.

Instead, they carry on conversations either in a superficial vein or in the vein of attack and defend. They either talk around what's important, or they do the parry-and-thrust of the big struggle.

Neither leads anywhere good.

Empathy, on the other hand, can break new ground.

Here is an example from our own marriage. One of my, Ned's, complaints about Sue is that she is *too nice*. She always understands the other person's point of view and she is almost never judgmental. She really believes that to understand all is to forgive all.

Sometimes this drives me nuts. One summer day when we were driving back home from a week on Cape Cod, we were stuck in horrible traffic. Suddenly we heard a siren fast approaching, so we, like everyone else, pulled over to let the ambulance through. Just as the ambulance zipped past us, a car in front of us pulled out and started to follow the ambulance.

"What a jerk!" Sue said. Then almost immediately she took it back and said, "But who knows, maybe it was that guy's father who was in the ambulance."

I sputtered in exasperation, "Sue, why can't you just call him a jerk and leave it at that? Why do you have to make excuses for him? Do you really think that guy could see into the darkened back window of a speeding ambulance and identify his father?"

Sue laughed and said of course not. But then she asked me, "Why does it bother you so much when I do this?"

Had I been feeling defensive, I could have taken that question as an invitation to a struggle. Instead, I stopped and thought for a few moments. I had never seriously reflected on why, in fact, it does bother me so much that Sue can't be mean, that she can't call someone a jerk, that she always has to see the other point of view.

As I thought about it, I came up with a reason why. Growing up, I never had a stable set of parents, and I got sent away to a boarding school in the fifth grade. I pretty much grew up in boarding schools.

So I said to Sue, "I think the reason it bothers me so much is that I never had someone when I was growing up who could get angry at someone on my behalf. I never had a strong parent. I never had someone who would go into school or go to someone's house or go to anyone and pound the table or raise hell on my behalf. I had to do it all on my own, and I wish to this day that someone else would stand up and fight for me. I think that's why I'd love to see you ream someone out. Does that make sense?"

"It makes perfect sense," Sue said. "Thanks."

Since then, I've not felt nearly as annoyed when Sue is so very nice because I understand that my intensely negative reaction derives from something I didn't get growing up, not with Sue being too nice. In fact, as flaws go, being too nice is a pretty good one to have.

But we have also discussed what happened in Sue's life that has made it so important to her that people get along with each other and that people approve of her. She is not quite as open as I am about revealing personal details of her life in books, so we won't go into detail here. The important point is that the work of understanding, the work of developing useful and true empathy, requires time, attention, and thought. You certainly do not have to have a degree in psychology to do this. All you must have is a keen desire to understand the other person.

Where does such interest in knowing another person come from? Romantic love is sometimes based on *not* knowing the other person, on denying faults and flaws. But, as you mature as a couple, it becomes more and more difficult to simply deny what is annoying. When you reach this juncture, you have a choice to make. You can enter the attack-and-defend mode where many couples spend most of their lives together, or you can choose to understand the other person.

Thus the motivation to develop empathy comes from your wanting a better life for yourself! The attack-and-defend mode is so unpleasant that it's well worth the time and patience it takes to understand why your mate is the way he or she is.

Once you understand, really understand, it becomes far more difficult to attack your mate. There is a lot of truth in the saying "To understand all is to forgive all."

But developing that understanding takes work. Fighting, living in the attack-and-defend mode, is easy. No work at all. Just easy misery. It's toxic, but at some primitive level, fighting even feels good for a few moments. That's one reason it's so common. People like to fight.

To make progress you must forgo that pleasure. Learn to understand, without sitting in judgment. Unlike fighting, this is *not* easy. It takes forbearance. It is a cliché to say that relationships take work. We believe developing empathy is the heart of that work: learning how to listen, explore, and understand without letting your judgments get in the way.

Do you know how good it feels to have someone really want to know what you're feeling, really want to know what life is like from your subjective point of view, and not jump in with a judgment about it? It is one of the greatest feelings in the world. It is a hallmark of true love, often rhapsodized, but rarely practiced.

Yet, the tool of empathy resides within each of us, ready to be worked.

In this chapter, we have given you some of our ideas on how to work that tool and some sample questions you can ask each other. Fundamentally, working the tool of empathy requires that you shift from wanting to be right, or wanting to be safe, to wanting to understand. You must first of all be open-mindedly curious. You must, in a sense, be ignorant of the other person . . . but eager to learn.

"Teach me," should be your supplication. "Teach me who you are."

Part 2

RESOLVING THE PROBLEMS
OF DISTRACTION

EIGHT

Struggle Stoppers

Man is sometimes extraordinarily, passionately, in love with suffering.

—FYODOR DOSTOYEVSKY

Unless you are like Dostoyevsky's character in *Notes from Underground,* you want to put an end to pain in your life. In marriage, stupid struggles are usually a main source of pain. In the previous chapter, we recommended empathy and understanding as the chief means of curtailing struggles. The more two people know and understand each other, the easier it becomes to see what's going on beneath the struggle and to get out of the damaging pattern of attack and defend, defend and attack.

In this section of the book, we take the process of dismantling struggles a bit further.

Remember, if you are married to distraction, you will never be able to end the struggles until you both take the time to pay attention. Attention is the often forgotten, obvious sine qua non of empathy, understanding, and putting an end to struggles. But attention requires time. So the first struggle stopper is simply this: make time, regularly, to pay attention to the person you love.

If you are not tuned in to the other person, if you're unaware of what he or she is going through, you are far more apt to get into a struggle. This is obvious, but worth stating because it is so often forgotten. For example, if I come home in a grumpy mood and have no clue as to what Sue has put up with during the day, if she says anything but "Welcome home, my love!" I am liable to feel rebuffed and respond with some curt remark. And so the struggle starts.

Since distraction is a prime obstacle to empathy, distraction itself promotes struggles. You can't tune in to another person if you yourself are distracted. That's one reason so many struggles begin around stupid stuff. People start fighting because they are tuned in to their own frustrated, grumpy moods and are clueless to the other person's state of mind.

Distraction blocks empathy. Lack of empathy sets the stage for a fight. So the first and most important struggle stopper is to take the time to tune in to the other person, even if you are in a bad place yourself.

The next struggle stopper is to avoid getting tangled up in the substance and content of the argument. The stated content of most arguments and struggles is silly. Here are some common examples:

EXAMPLE 1

"We're lost. Why can't you ever get good directions?"

"Why is it up to me to get directions? You're driving!"

"Yes, and since I am driving, you take the responsibility of being the navigator."

"Says who? You always make up the rules as you go along."

"No, that's not true. What is true is that you resent anyone but you having any bit of control."

"I want control? That coming from Mr. Control Freak himself! Are you joking?"

EXAMPLE 2

"There's a stop sign ahead."

"I can see the stop sign perfectly well."

"I'm just trying to help."

"By pointing out every stop sign?"

"What if you didn't see it? Wouldn't it be better if I pointed it out?"

"I'm not blind!"

"And I'm not deaf. You don't have to yell at me."

"Well, it just pisses me off when you treat me like some kind of imbecile. I know how to drive."

"And it makes me angry when you act like some macho man who isn't willing to accept any help."

"Help I don't need is insulting."

"You are way too easily insulted."

EXAMPLE 3

"Julie overdrew her account again. I don't know what to do with her."

"She's only seventeen years old. I'll put some more money in her account."

"That's a bad idea. How is she going to learn to be responsible with money if you always bail her out?"

"I'll talk to her about being more careful."

"And you think that will work? She needs consequences."

"I think I can give her guidance. I think that works better."

"You really spoil her, you know."

"I don't think so. I think you are in a competition with her and that makes you too harsh on her."

"Wow, that's a zinger. Where did you come up with that?"

EXAMPLE 4

"The Browns want us to come for dinner Saturday."

"No, I'm tired. Let's not."

"You're tired? But today is Tuesday. Are you saying you'll be tired Saturday?"

"I'm saying I'm tired of going out. I just want to stay home and relax."

"How about what I want to do?"

"You always want to go out. And we go out a lot."

"Your idea of a lot and my idea of a lot are quite different."

"No kidding! Just look at our sex life."

———

Each of the examples begins with some trivial issue but quickly escalates into something major, even hurtful. The problem in each of these examples, and with most couples where struggles are common, is that both members of the couple are spoiling for a fight. Any little provocation can quickly lead to an explosion.

Don't mistake the content of the argument for the cause of the argument. You can waste hours, even years, debating an issue on its merits, on its content, but never bring an end to the argument because the content, the issue, was not the cause or the driving force in the first place. The cause of the struggle, usually, has almost nothing to do with the content of the argument.

Because the struggle so rarely stems from the content, the remedy is not to be found in learning how to argue fairly, or in taking a course in successful negotiation, or in learning to bite your tongue. Those kinds of remedies miss the underlying cause.

The underlying cause is most often a feeling of being insufficiently loved, respected, or tended to. In today's crazy-busy, distracted world, couples commonly feel a lack of love from the other. It is also common when there is more to do than time to do it, when people are overloaded, that civility declines, even between people who love each other, so that each member of the couple feels disrespected.

Most of the time, ongoing conflict in couples is driven by a feeling of deprivation, a feeling that *I am not getting what I need, want, and deserve.* That leads the couple to lash out at each other, which of course intensifies the feelings of deprivation.

A vicious cycle sets in. Person A and person B have not been paying much attention to each other. Person A starts to feel unloved, so she attacks B. B, who also feels unloved, reacts by attacking back, which makes A feel even more unloved, which leads her to attack B even more harshly, which, naturally, leads to a nasty counterattack by B upon A. And so it can go, often for years on end.

Unfortunately, due to pride or even simple lack of awareness of true feelings, people don't come right out and say, "I feel neglected. I need more from you."

If you can learn to speak those simple, straightforward words, you can prevent many struggles. And when you hear those words, if you can learn not to react defensively, you can avoid even more struggles.

A famous skit on the Bob Newhart TV show sums up nicely how we, as therapists, often wish we could resolve this struggle. It goes something like this:

PATIENT: Doctor, I worry about everything. Everywhere I go, in everything I do, I worry incessantly, even though I know my worries are ridiculous and that my life is wonderful, except for my worrying.

NEWHART: Yes, I have seen this problem before. I have a cure for you. The cure is just two words.

PATIENT: Oh, wonderful! Let me get a pen and paper and write these words down.

NEWHART: No, I don't think you'll need pen and paper. I'm pretty sure you will remember these two words without needing to write them down.

PATIENT: All right, Doctor. Tell me, then, what are these two words?

NEWHART: The next time you worry, remember the following two words: *Stop it!*

How we wish we could say to couples who are struggling day in and day out, *"Stop it!"* Of course, we *could* say that, but the chances of their being able to follow the advice would be pretty slim. That's because the underlying cause—feelings of deprivation—can't be fixed by being suppressed.

On the other hand, you *can* learn to curtail your struggles by using a method not terribly more complicated. You need to state your feelings in a nonaccusing or sarcastic way. Here's how the conversation might go:

"I don't want to make you feel bad, but I just don't feel much love from you lately. It's getting me down. I don't want to become bitchy all the time, but that's usually what happens when I feel neglected."

"I know. I've been really under the gun at work, and you're right, I haven't been there for you, or the kids either, for that matter. I'm sorry."

"Just acknowledging it and saying you're sorry helps. But is there any chance we might get some time together soon?"

"Work has been hell. They want more from me this weekend. But time with you is as good for me as it is for you, so screw work. I will take Saturday evening and do whatever you'd like to do."

"Anything?"

"I like that look in your eye. Haven't seen it in a while. Yes, anything. Surprise me."

———

When it comes to struggle stoppers, prevention tops the list. If you can speak your feelings, openly and simply, and if your partner can listen and empathize without getting defensive, you can stave off most struggles.

Struggles and fights usually emerge out of a feeling of deprivation; one or both members of the couple feel short on something. The "something" might be:

- love
- attention
- sex
- money
- respect
- control
- time
- power
- freedom
- variety
- adventure, excitement
- sleep
- leisure time

- time with friends
- career fulfillment
- vacation
- material wants
- time with extended family

The list could go on and on. The point is to learn the habit of asking yourself, *Of what do I feel deprived? What am I not getting that I need?* Speak that need *before* you start to argue, fight, or get the need met somewhere else.

Don't make the mistake that most couples make of getting entangled in the substance of the struggle. Instead, look at the context in which it occurs. Look for the deprivation and address that.

For example, if you are arguing over child-rearing practices as Julie's parents were in example #3 and getting nowhere, try not to get all tangled up in the issues of the argument. Instead, step back and ask, "Why are we fighting like this? Is it just because you think I spoil Julie and I think you are too harsh on her? Or are we both feeling kind of disappointed in ourselves?"

Here the deprivation might be of self-esteem. When Julie overdrew the account, each parent felt responsible and inadequate. They ended up lashing out at each other instead of acknowledging the underlying feeling, which was, for each, one of not being a good enough parent.

In addition to feelings of deprivation, another common source of struggle is hurt feelings, which lead to a desire for revenge. When you feel hurt, it is human nature to want to hurt back. This is one of the basic Laws of Human Nature: *for every hurt, people seek an equal and opposite hurt.* You could write a history of the world based on that one law. Sadly, you could write the history of most marriages that ended in divorce based on that one law as well.

Instead of obeying that law, when you feel hurt, try asking yourself the following question: *What do I want my pain to turn into?*

Your first reply will be "I want him to hurt just as much as I do, preferably more!" You can see how that feeling could launch you into a struggle that might last for years. Hurt follows hurt follows hurt. If you're not careful, that cycle can rule your entire relationship.

This kind of struggle feeds on each person's desire to be right. "She deserves to suffer because she was entirely in the wrong." Each party invests his or her energy and intellect in justifying his or her position.

"Your flirting with that woman at the party was a direct insult to me."

"You're just too jealous. I didn't flirt with her at all. You are too possessive and insecure, and that totally clouds your judgment."

"Do you deny you were flirting with her? It was so obvious to me and everyone else."

"Oh, did you discuss it with 'everyone else'? Did you take a poll? Did you go around and ask people, 'Is my husband flirting?' I doubt that. But I wish you had because you would have seen how paranoid you are."

"Okay, the next time we're out together, I'll give you a taste of your own medicine and we'll see how secure and confident you are. As I recall, you don't exactly love it when I pay attention to other men. I am really looking forward to this."

"Oh, so you're looking forward to doing something that you know will hurt me and upset me. That's really mature."

"About as mature as your flirting with that little scamp and not being able to admit to it."

"I can't stand this feeling of control and jealousy. I can't stand how you want to keep me on a leash."

"And I can't believe what a totally selfish person you are."

———

Back and forth it goes, attack and defend. The wife felt hurt and she responded by attacking her husband. In turn, he felt defensive and attacked back. This led the wife to threaten revenge, which led to more attacks by the husband.

The way out of this vicious cycle is for one or both members of the couple to ask, *What do I want my pain to turn into?* While the immediate reaction might be "More pain!" that would not be your response upon wise reflection. You would want your pain to turn into an end of pain, into growth, into deeper understanding. Guided by those principles, the conversation above could have gone like this:

"I thought you were flirting with that woman at the party. I felt really upset and put off by it. Don't you find me exciting?"

"I honestly wasn't flirting. I was just being friendly. You are a hundred times more attractive than she is. I am very happy with you. I love you."

"But it seemed like you were paying a lot of attention to her, touching her hands, staring into her eyes, ignoring everyone else."

"Honey, you're seeing more in it than was there. I talked to her for maybe five minutes. But I'm really sorry to have hurt you. You honestly have no reason to feel insecure. You're the only woman in the world I want."

"I don't think I'm insecure. I just don't like seeing you pay attention to other women."

"Do you know why this is such a hot-button issue for you?"

"It is for most women, I think."

"But it's especially so for you. Did someone cheat on you that you haven't told me about?"

"Only my father. On my mom."

"You've mentioned something about that before, but only in passing, like it was not that big of a deal."

"I know. It isn't my favorite topic. It *was* a big deal. It happened so often. And she would turn to me for help. It was impossible. I hated it all. I don't want to talk about it now."

"I'm really sorry. I'm sorry you had to go through that. I understand things a lot better now."

———

Again, taking the time to develop empathy can not only sidestep an unnecessary argument but break new ground for understanding. In this instance, instead of looking for revenge, both people moved beyond that. Instead of turning pain into more pain, they turned pain into understanding and growth.

The desire for revenge is one of the most universal and harmful of all human reactions. It is seductive because a person believes that revenge will in some way make the situation better. But it only makes it worse, most of the time. Feuds begin. Long-standing struggles become all but institutionalized in families. People waste quantities of mental energy in plotting and scheming, justifying and arguing, sometimes suing, and almost always making life bitter and unpleasant.

Seeking revenge is like swallowing poison and expecting the other person to die.

Instead, learn to forgive. By forgive, we do not mean that you condone the bad thing that hurt you; we do not mean that you should behave like a doormat and invite further mistreatment; we do not mean that you turn the other cheek. By forgive, we simply mean that you get past the hold that anger and resentment have upon you. You free yourself of ongoing anger and resentment and the search for revenge those feelings beget. You free *yourself*. In this sense, forgiveness is a gift you give not mainly to the other person, but to yourself. And to the relationship.

Freeing yourself of anger and resentment isn't easy. It can take weeks, even years if the hurt goes deep. But you are far better heading toward forgiveness than heading toward revenge and the nursing of a grudge.

If you'd like some help in learning how to forgive, you might want to read a book that Ned wrote called *Dare to Forgive*. The book describes a reliable method you can use to get past anger and resentment. It also offers many true examples—some of minor acts of forgiveness, some of major acts of forgiveness—that demonstrate the various ways a person can get past chronic anger and resentment and find the peace and renewed energy that forgiveness invariably brings.

Some struggles or arguments are inevitable. In fact, if a couple never argues, they are either amazingly well matched or at least one of them is suppressing his or her true voice and will. It is not healthy for couples never to disagree, never to argue, never to struggle, because it means they are unable to contend and compete for desired outcomes, be they trivial desired outcomes, such as what to watch on TV, or major desired outcomes, such as what house to buy, what religion (if any) to join, or how to intervene in a child's life.

But when the struggles become chronic, they become destructive.

You should find a way to stop them before they stop you. Here is a summary of the struggle stoppers we recommend:

1. Spend time together.
2. Pay attention to one another.
3. Understand yourself and your partner well enough that you can see what lies beneath the struggle.
4. Speak your true feelings.
5. Know when you feel deprived and speak that feeling.
6. When you feel hurt by the other person, ask yourself, "What do I want this pain to turn into?" Try to rise above that very human tendency to return pain with pain.
7. Practice preventive maintenance. Have special times together every week. Even if it is just for a few minutes, try to make your partner feel special.
8. When a fight is about to escalate, ask yourself, "Is this worth it?"
9. Remember, your effort to be right might include making the other person be wrong, which is humiliating. In a marriage, being right is far less important than being kind.
10. Seeing a good therapist can make a huge difference. In our experience, social workers make the best couples therapists. And we're not just saying that because Sue is one! But, of course, any mental health professional or other kind of counselor can make a good couples therapist. The best way to choose a therapist is to get a recommendation from someone you trust who has seen the therapist and had a positive experience. The next best way is to get a referral from your primary-care doctor. Once you have selected a therapist, trust your gut. If, after a session or two, you just do not feel as if you have established a good connection, then seek another therapist. Often, patients feel they ought to stick it out for months and months. This is usually a waste of time and money. Instead, keep looking until you find the right therapist for you and your partner.

NINE

Download Overload

The world is too much with us; late and soon,
Getting and spending, we lay waste our powers;
Little we see in Nature that is ours;
We have given our hearts away, a sordid boon!
—WILLIAM WORDSWORTH, 1807

Imagine what Wordsworth would write today!

Since the force of distraction is so powerful, ubiquitous, and corrosive in relationships, and since mental overload has a similarly negative effect in that it makes people irritable, seemingly selfish, and unsympathetic, we use this chapter to offer some more specific tips on how to fight these forces.

1. TIO. Turn it off. That should be one of the Ten Commandments of Relationships in Modern Life. Cell phone, computer, BlackBerry, iPod, television, laptop, whatever it might be, turn

it off. Distraction and overload will subside the instant you do this. Rarely is one intervention so simple yet so effective.

2. Learn to say "No" or "Let me get back to you on that." Make no your default response, the response you automatically give first. You can learn to say no politely. You can't let your default position be yes unless you want to be totally swamped.

3. Cut back on screensucking. *Screensucking* is my term for mindless time spent online, sending and receiving meaningless emails, surfing the Net, letting the time pass as nothing of any import transpires. This can become a sinkhole for your time. Screensucking in turn leads you to feel overloaded as you do not have time to do what you need to get done.

4. Meditate or pray. Mindfulness practices, such as meditation or prayer, refurbish your ability to focus and replenish your stores of attention.

5. Close the door. Spend some time alone with your partner.

6. Have a date night. You'd be amazed what one night out a week can do to reestablish closeness and connection. But you must do it regularly. Once a year won't work.

7. Schedule sex. Sounds unromantic? It's a lot more romantic than not having sex. Plus, anticipation is a kind of foreplay. If you know that at 10 p.m. on Tuesday you will make love, the days leading up to Tuesday can become more exciting.

8. Prioritize. Know what matters most to you and do it. So simple. But many people when asked the question "What matters most to you?" have no reply. If you do not know what matters most to you, it is difficult to protect it!

9. Curtail. Cut back on what you have too much of to do. Imagine your life is a garden you want to love, but it has become overrun with thickets and weeds. You take out your pruning shears and *cut back*. Once you get started, it will feel really good. And you'll love your garden once again.

10. Delegate. Get others to do what you are bad at or dislike. You can trade off, you can hire out, you can persuade. However you do it, delegate what you don't like or are bad at. You will feel far less overloaded if you are mostly doing what you like and what you're good at.

11. Eliminate. Cut out obligations, activities, even people that drain you. When you eliminate something, don't immediately replace it with something else.

12. Put a message on your voice mail explaining when you return messages. Do not feel you must return every message every day. Otherwise, you can spend your time doing little else.

13. Also, put a note on your emails explaining when you return emails. Explain how much depth—or lack thereof—you have time to go into in emails.

14. Let people know that if they want to have a meaningful conversation with you, it is best done in person.

15. Preserve what we call the "human moment," time spent face-to-face. Don't let electronic moments replace it.

16. Resist the temptation always to be *doing* something—reading something, watching something, talking into something. We often court the force of distraction. What then happens is, we spend almost no time thinking.

17. Get regular physical exercise. Exercise is not only good for your body, it is great for your mind. When you exercise, your body puts out powerful chemicals that act as antidepressants, antianxiety agents, antistressors, mind-focusers, and mood enhancers.

18. Instead of always having the radio or TV on when you're alone, *learn to listen to your own thoughts.* People can become so accustomed always to having some sort of electronic "muzak" playing, they forget what it is like to entertain their own thoughts. Then, one day, they don't have any anymore.

19. Unsubscribe to some magazine or list-serve.

20. Don't always keep up with the news, unless your job depends upon it. The news is a prime source of distraction and feelings of overload.

21. Get rid of "leeches": people or projects that waste your time. People stay with leeches usually out of inertia or guilt. These are bad reasons to give away your time.

22. Cultivate lilies. The opposite of leeches, lilies are people or projects that are worth your time, people or projects that repay the effort you put in. Our favorite example of lilies are our

kids. Whatever yours are, cultivate them! You will feel fulfilled every day.

23. Have a creative outlet. Creative activity naturally screens out the force of distraction. Make time for whatever your creative juices lead you to do, from cooking, to painting, to devising a new business plan.

24. Protect and use your "morning burst." *Morning burst* is our term for the time during the day when you are freshest. For most people, this is in the morning. For some it is at night. And for others, it is midday. It lasts about an hour, maybe less. Don't squander your morning burst on email or watching television. Talk with your mate, play with your kids, work on an important project. Just don't waste this precious time on trivial stuff.

25. Be real. Let your true self come out. People wear themselves out being "appropriate," censoring themselves, keeping their spontaneous selves under wraps. This is counterproductive and draining. Relax. Be real. Once you get in the habit, you'll feel much more peppy and alive and your relationships will benefit.

TEN

Eliminate Toxic Worry

We have emphasized the importance of positive factors—time, attention, empathy, connection, and play—in promoting intimacy and combating the forces of distraction in today's world. However, one negative factor is so prevalent and so poisonous to intimacy that it warrants discussion on its own: toxic worry.

If you worry more today than you did a decade ago, you're not alone.

Everyone's worry has ramped up. But why? What has happened? While worry and anxiety are partially created by our genes—some people are born to worry, while others are born cool as a cucumber— our gene pool hasn't changed in the past decade, so we can't look to genetics for the answer. Could it be that the number of catastrophic, or potentially catastrophic, events modern life has foisted upon us is what has led to this age of worry? There are so many. . . . We won't depress you with a list you already know only too well. Suffice it to say, there are many, the collapse of the economy perhaps heading the list.

But if you pulled up a random year from the Dark Ages, you could probably find as much, if not more, to worry about. It's impossible to know how worried people were back then, but our sense is they weren't as nervous as we've become. Maybe they just expected less from life. We do have great expectations, and that may contribute to our high levels of worry.

But I think our high anxiety has a uniquely modern cause. As Thomas Friedman says, the world is now flat. We're all connected electronically with few barriers of time or space between us. That's great, except when it isn't.

As we've mentioned, at the core of our electronic matrix lies a paradox. While they've been connecting electronically, many people have disconnected interpersonally.

As a person disconnects interpersonally, he tends to worry. The more isolated a person becomes, the more worried, even paranoid, he usually gets. We believe the spike in toxic worry we see today derives not so much from the problems of the world—problems have always beset us—but from our relative disconnection from each other. The effect on a marriage can be acute.

A person who is married to distraction is at risk to become married to worry as well. Here's how the vicious cycle runs:

STEP 1. A person becomes distracted.
STEP 2. Distraction gradually leads to disconnection from intimate engagement.
STEP 3. Disconnection from such support begets toxic worry.
STEP 4. Worry itself becomes a preoccupying distraction.
STEP 5. Such distraction intensifies the disconnection.
STEP 6. The ongoing disconnection intensifies the worry.

And on the cycle runs.

So what is to be done? We have a four-step plan that allows you to eliminate 90 percent of toxic worry from your life without the use of medication. Here it is.

Step one is the most important. It is to connect with a person you trust and like. As an old teacher of ours used to say, "It is fine to worry, just never worry alone!" Worrying alone intensifies the worry. Worrying with a friend usually converts the worry into good worry. Don't turn away from your intimate partner when you are worried. Turn to her. Turn to him.

Think of how you feel if you are alone in the dark in a huge room. You feel frightened, even paranoid. But if you are in that same room in the dark with a friend, you feel less fear. Your feeling of vulnerability all but disappears. You feel in control.

Modern life has ushered in such a raft of worry because so many people are worrying alone. Most of the tragedies such as Columbine that leave people wondering how this could happen share one cause: human disconnection. People who feel alone and rejected do bad things.

At a more superficial level, if you get in the habit of sharing your worries with people you like and respect, you will rarely suffer toxic worry for any significant amount of time, and you will rarely feel overcome in your imagination by the stresses of life.

Step two in this process is to *get the facts*. Toxic worry is usually based on wrong information or lack of information. If you see a mole on your forearm, *go to the doctor*, don't just brood and worry that you have a melanoma. If your business is in trouble, *hire a consultant*. Don't just imagine doom. And if your marriage is in trouble, *talk with your spouse*, don't isolate yourself in angry, lonely, worried thinking. Let your mate become your chief ally in getting the facts. He or she may not have the facts, but can offer you the encouragement you need to get them.

Step three is *make a plan*. It follows logically from step two. Once you have the facts, or as many of the facts as you can get, put a plan together. It doesn't matter if the plan fails. Then you just revise the plan. Life is all about revising plans that didn't work. The key is to stay in the active mode. Toxic worry feasts on a passive person like a buzzard feasts on a fallen animal. Brainstorm with your mate to make plans. Don't hunker down on your own. Stay connected and in an active, planning mode.

When you have a plan, you automatically feel more powerful and less vulnerable. You automatically feel more optimistic and upbeat. Toxic worry subsides. And you feel closer to your mate. You have not allowed the vicious cycle to divide you.

Finally, step four is *let it go*. Many toxic worriers clutch their worries and can't let them go. It is as if they feel it were bad luck not to worry. As long as they suffer the pain of toxic worry, they feel magically protected. They fear if they let the worry go, some bad thing will happen. This is, of course, nonsense. As long as you have gone through steps one through three, it is safe to let the worry go. You've done what you can. Now it is time to move on to some other project or topic. Not only will this help you, it will help your relationship as well.

————

We said our plan would take care of 90 percent of your toxic worry, but what about the 10 percent it doesn't fix? And what if toxic worry in you or your spouse is making your marriage difficult if not unbearable?

This is where modern psychiatry can really help. True anxiety disorders are no joke. They can torture a person daily. Obsessive-compulsive disorder (OCD), generalized anxiety disorder, panic attacks, social phobias, and post-traumatic stress disorder, to name some of the most common of these, can cripple a person.

For these conditions, the four-step plan will not be enough. You ought to consult a mental health professional or urge your spouse to do so. You can't make the diagnosis yourself, but if you find that toxic worry just won't go away, if you are held back in your work and your relationships by chronic worry, then you should consult with a mental health professional. You might consult with a social worker, a psychologist, a psychiatrist, a nurse practitioner, or you might start with your primary-care physician. But do seek help.

Often, people who suffer from chronic forms of toxic worry don't want to go for help. They are too anxious to talk about the problem. Or they fear the help will be useless. Or they see their condition as a form of weakness and feel shame. That's why often their spouse needs to urge them to get help and accompany them to the first appointment.

The help you will get might include medication, but it might not. We now have a wide array of treatments for anxiety and worry, many of which are natural and do not involve medications. The medications we now have are safe and effective, as long as they are prescribed properly and supervised.

Whatever treatment you get, make sure you like the professional you are seeing. No matter what the treatment might be, it will be far more effective if you like and trust the person who is providing it. It is worth looking around to find the right practitioner. You will be discussing highly personal issues. It is important that you feel comfortable doing so. Much of the benefit from the treatment derives from the relationship you make with the practitioner. Make sure it is positive and harmonious.

However you do it, quelling toxic worry, such a common phenomenon in today's distracted world, can save a relationship.

ELEVEN

When Your Spouse Has True ADD

Mary comes home to find her husband, Joel, sitting at the kitchen table doing a jigsaw puzzle with a puzzle piece sticking out of his mouth. Joel looks up at her. The puzzle piece makes him look absurd. Mary bursts into tears.

Taking the piece out of his mouth, Joel quickly says, "Honey, hold on, it's not what you think. I've been looking for work all day. I've sent out three résumés. I called Maria, and she said she could coach me tomorrow. I only started on the puzzle an hour ago. I did the food shopping first, and I started the laundry. Dinner is actually in the oven."

"And where's the car, Joel?" Mary asks, wiping away tears.

"In the driveway, where I left it."

"In the driveway where you left it?"

"Yes. What, you mean it isn't there?"

"It's there. It's there all right. How long ago did you leave it there?"

"I left it when I got back from shopping. Four or five hours ago.

What's wrong? Did you want me to park it somewhere else? What's *wrong*, Mary?"

" *You're* what's wrong, Joel. I don't know how else to put it anymore. You're what's wrong." Mary goes to the refrigerator and takes out a bottle of wine. She pours herself a glass of pinot grigio and drinks it down. Then she pours another.

"Can you bring me a beer, hon?" Joel asks.

"I don't know why I'm bringing you a beer," Mary says, handing Joel his Heineken. "Maybe it's because you still call me hon. But I could kill you. Do you know that that car, which, as you said, you did park in the driveway, *is still running*? Do you know that you just got out of that car and left it there, key in the ignition with the engine running? It's a miracle no one stole it. I didn't turn it off because I wanted you to see it for yourself and believe what you did. Why don't you go check it out before you drink your beer?"

Joel has already bolted from the table and is out the door. In a couple of minutes he walks slowly back in. "I can't believe I did that," he says softly, sitting back down at the table with Mary.

"You can't?" Mary exclaims. "Why not? I sure can. In fact, I'm surprised you don't do it every day. You simply have no clue how clueless you are."

"Thanks, hon."

"Ah, sarcasm. When all else fails."

"I'm sorry, Mary. What else can I say?"

"Oh, Joel, I'm sorry, too. I'm so very sorry. I love you, honestly I do, but you are making me crazy. I don't like who I am becoming with you. I'm like an angry parent, trying to ride herd on a boy who just can't get his act together. But you're my husband! What am I supposed to do? Just keep picking up after you, reminding you to say hello to people and say good-bye, reminding you whose name is whose, reminding you to brush your teeth and change your shirt and call your mother and buy *me* a birthday present? I'm worn-out. You're wearing me out. This life is wearing me out. I have to support us financially, raise the kids, plus do everything else. While you do jigsaw puzzles and put pieces in your mouth."

"That's not fair," Joel says. "I told you what I did today."

Mary sighs. "Good for you. Good for you." Then she starts to cry again.

"What am I supposed to do? I'm doing my best to find a job. This is not a good time to be looking. And I'm taking care of the house during the day, picking the kids up, playing with them, getting them started on their homework . . ."

"I know you think you're doing all that. But do you know how much of it I have to redo or fix when I get home? I don't mean to sound like a bitch, and I don't want to make you feel worse than you already do, it's just that I can't take it anymore. I spoke to a lawyer today."

"About a divorce?" Joel said, with horror on his face.

"No, I went and spoke to a lawyer about my tennis serve. Of course, it was about a divorce. What else would I talk to a lawyer about? But don't worry. We just had a conversation. I needed to know what my options are and what the kids' options are. Life simply can't go on like this. You are the most talented man I know, Joel, you are the only man I have ever truly loved, you are the father of my children and the love of my life, but you are killing me. You're killing us. I can't stand to see you waste your talent and also make my life into this . . . this constant mess, this chaos, this misery. I want to scream at you all the time . . . and that's no way to live . . . for me or for you."

"But I love you, Mary. I need you."

"I know you need me, Joel. That's the whole problem. You need me too much. And I don't need you at all. I'd love to need you, but I've learned not to need you because I can't rely on you. I'm sorry. I just don't see how we can make a good life for each other and the kids."

———

It sounds hopeless, but it may not be. Before they get a divorce, Mary and Joel ought to see a therapist who understands attention deficit disorder, or ADD (it is technically called attention-deficit/hyperactivity disorder, or ADHD, but we call it ADD since that is the name most people recognize and understand). Many of the telltale signs of ADD stand out in their conversation. If Joel does have ADD, the right intervention could save the marriage.

As a specialist in ADD for nearly thirty years, I, Ned, have seen many couples who were on the brink of divorce preserve their marriage through understanding and treating ADD. Untreated ADD can be devastating. But, with proper treatment, everything can change.

I have written books on ADD, which I will not recap here. If you want to learn more, I urge you to read *Delivered from Distraction,* my most recent book on ADD in adults (written with John Ratey). But to help you determine if it would be worthwhile for you to look into the possibility that you or your spouse might have ADD, here is a quick summary of the salient characteristics of the condition.

1. Unexplained underachievement. Adults who have ADD typically achieve inconsistently. Some days they are brilliant. Other days they are the opposite. Like Joel, they exasperate people because they seem to be wasting their talent for no good reason. The pattern leads bosses and spouses to believe they are not trying hard enough on those days when they perform poorly. But it is not a matter of effort. The inconsistency in performance results from inconsistency of mental focus, which in turns results from genetics, from how they are wired.

2. Easy distractibility, coupled with an ability to hyperfocus, like a laser beam, at times. This is the hallmark symptom of ADD. The person inadvertently, unintentionally tunes out in the middle of a page or a conversation. The mind does not go empty, it goes elsewhere. Attention deficit is a misnomer. It is attention wandering. The ADD mind is like a toddler on a picnic. It goes where curiosity leads it, regardless of danger, rules, or the expectations of other people. When it finds an object of interest, it focuses intently. It just may not be where it is "supposed" to focus.

3. Trouble with time management. People with ADD have a different sense of time from other people. In the world of ADD, there are only two times: *now* and *not now.* As a result, the person with ADD procrastinates, putting things off until the last minute. At the last minute, not now becomes now. Then, in a panic, the person swings into action. Inadvertently, he uses his panic as self-medication, because when you panic, you secrete

adrenaline, which is chemically similar to the stimulant medications (such as Ritalin, Concerta, Adderall, Vyvanse, and Dexedrine) that we use to treat ADD. Adrenaline is like nature's own stimulant medication.

4. Tendency to be impulsive and creative. People with ADD often act first, think later. This can get them into all sorts of trouble. However, this impulsivity has an upside: creativity. You cannot be creative if you are not somewhat spontaneous and disinhibited, which is to say, impulsive. You cannot plan to have a creative idea and say to yourself, "It's ten a.m., time for my creative thought," then lay it like an egg. No, creative thoughts come unbidden. They are often intrusive and distracting. You can see why ADD and creativity go hand in hand.

5. Search for high stimulation. People with ADD *hate* to be bored. No one likes to be bored, but for a person with ADD, boredom is like an intense muscle cramp. It must immediately be relieved. So, people with ADD look for situations that are high on stimulation and low on routine. They tend to go into such fields as criminal law, surgery, car racing, acting, cowboying, news reporting, entrepreneurial ventures, trading on the commodities exchanges, flying airplanes, sales, bull riding . . . anything that is highly engaging, leaves lots of room for independence, is unpredictable, includes a dash of danger, and allows the person to feel free.

6. An insistence on being free. Tendency to be resolutely independent.

7. Tendency to be impatient. Cut to the chase. Get to the bottom line. A romantic conversation with an adult who has ADD can go like this: "Okay, so you love me, now what's your next point?" People with ADD have a difficult time lingering over anything, even if the subject is something pleasant, such as being loved.

8. Tendency to be stubborn. Tendency to want to do whatever it is your way. When all else fails, the person with ADD *might* read the directions.

9. Problems with organization, planning, prioritizing, and acting

in a logical sequence of steps. The ADD person's desk, office, bedroom, or car often looks as if a tornado just passed through. Often the least important detail gets the most attention, while the most important task gets overlooked altogether (think of Joel leaving his car running). Plans get made but get changed in a heartbeat. To people with ADD a plan feels more like an encumbrance than an aid (even though when they follow a plan, they often feel greatly relieved). One of the many paradoxes in the world of ADD is that people with ADD do far better when they have structure, but they resist it as if it were going to imprison them.

10. Tendency to self-medicate with alcohol or other drugs, or with compulsive activities such as gambling, sex, spending, eating, or the newest addiction, electronics. A large percentage of people who have substance-abuse issues, or use other forms of self-medication, have untreated ADD. If they can get diagnosed and put on the right medication, i.e., a prescribed stimulant, then it becomes far easier for them to give up their drug or activity of abuse.

11. Mood instability. People with ADD have labile moods, which is to say their moods can change rapidly and without apparent cause. This is different from the oceanic, cycling mood shifts seen in bipolar disorder.

12. Tendency to worry needlessly. People with ADD often search for something to worry about. It is never hard to find something to worry about in any person's life. Once the target of worry is found, the person with ADD hyperfocuses on it and can't let go of it. It becomes an organizing principle. What the person is really looking for is focus. Nothing is more riveting than pain, and worry is mental pain. Unwittingly, the individual is using worry as a painful form of self-medication.

13. Problems with self-esteem. By the time the person with ADD becomes an adult, he or she has usually dealt with so many disappointments, so much inconsistent performance, so many reprimands and lectures to do better, that he or she feels defective, less than, and fundamentally flawed. This is one of the most tenacious and difficult to reverse of all the symptoms of

adult ADD. However, with treatment, most such adults can begin to cobble together a more positive sense of who they are.

14. High energy. Most adults with ADD have a lot of energy. They may not be hyperactive, physically, at all. But they usually have a great deal of mental, if not physical, energy.

15. Intuitive. People with ADD seem to have a sixth sense, an uncanny ability to see into problems and people. They have a knack for solving problems in business, science, interpersonal relations, or any other domain in which intuition can play a prominent role.

16. Sensitive. Goes along with intuitive. Adults with ADD tend to feel what others are feeling (when they are focused!). They can also easily be hurt, so they tend to cover their sensitivity.

17. Generous and bighearted. Often they are so generous, they have trouble looking out for their self-interest.

18. Trouble listening and following sequential instructions.

19. Tendency to have many projects going simultaneously, trouble with follow-through. Adults with ADD love beginnings. Middles tend to get boring.

20. Often a family history of ADD or genetically related conditions such as depression, bipolar disorder, substance abuse, disorders of impulse control, or anxiety disorders.

21. Coexisting conditions. Depression, anxiety, learning problems such as dyslexia, substance abuse, post-traumatic stress disorder, and other conditions often coexist with adult ADD. More often than not, treating the ADD greatly reduces, if not eliminates, these other conditions.

22. Life problems. Until the ADD gets diagnosed and treated, these adults tend to have trouble holding on to a job, staying in a marriage or other relationship, keeping up with friends, and following through on obligations. They are also accident-prone and have many more automobile accidents than the average person.

23. Various incidental findings. These are more common in adults with ADD than in the general population, but none may be present in a given adult with ADD. They include left-handedness or mixed dominance (which means you do some

tasks with one hand, other tasks with the other hand); childhood history of bed-wetting; thyroid dysfunction; childhood
history of many ear infections; migraine; allergies.

If you or your spouse see yourself in the traits listed above, then
run, don't walk, to get help. This diagnosis could save your marriage,
save your career, literally even save your life.

Read *Delivered from Distraction*, or some other book that teaches
you about ADD in adults. Learn all you can about adult ADD. Get
treatment from a professional who understands the condition and
won't just give you a medication, as if that were all that was needed.
The treatment should include education, identification of your talents
and strengths, counseling to help you make sense of the diagnosis and
explore the many emotions the diagnosis brings up, lifestyle changes,
coaching to help you get organized and develop a new game plan for
your marriage and career, and other interventions all tailored to bring
out the best in you.

For couples, often simply seeing the marriage and its problems
through the lens of ADD provides major relief. Let's say Joel, in the
example above, gets diagnosed with ADD. Once both Mary and Joel
learn about ADD, their dialogue could go like this:

MARY: This is so hard to believe. Why didn't someone tell us about
this sooner?

JOEL: I know. I've had this undiagnosed condition all my life. It's
cost me jobs, and it almost cost me you.

MARY: It's just amazing. I feel so guilty.

JOEL: It's not your fault. I don't blame you at all.

MARY: But the misery we've gone through, just because no one
made the right diagnosis.

JOEL: I know. But now we know what's going on. Life ought to improve a lot. I feel a lot better just knowing I'm not, you know, a
bad person.

MARY: You're a wonderful person. And now the wonderfulness can
come out.

JOEL: And I won't leave the car running in the driveway.

MARY: (Laughing) I know, can you believe that?

JOEL: Do I laugh or cry? To get to be forty-three years old and not know what's holding me back. At least I didn't give up. But I could have pounded my head against the same wall for the rest of my life.

MARY: No, you didn't give up. I almost did, though. I'm sorry.

JOEL: Don't be sorry. You were just looking out for the kids and yourself, and me, too, for that matter. It wasn't good, the way we were being with each other.

MARY: You are such a sweet man for being so understanding. We have a lot of making up to do.

JOEL: And I have a lot of work to do. I'm meeting with the coach tomorrow.

MARY: You like him? This is the new guy, right?

JOEL: The one Dr. Barton suggested. He says people have done well with him. Now that the meds are working the way they're supposed to, I ought to get a lot done. I'm excited, to tell you the truth. I haven't felt this positive in a long time.

MARY: I haven't heard you this positive in a long time, that's for sure. It sure feels good to be hopeful.

No, Mary and Joel will not fix their every problem, but they stand an excellent chance of creating a good life for themselves. Undiagnosed, ADD can ruin lives. But, once diagnosed, the positive attributes of ADD can soar to the surface and turn a nearly ruined life into that of a champion.

TWELVE

When Your Spouse Feels Like Your Child

Sometimes the person you married begins to feel not like a partner, coequal in your efforts to manage life, but a dependent, almost like a child. Many spouses have complained to us, "I can deal with the three children we have, but when my husband feels like a fourth child, I just can't take it."

This common problem grows out of the division of labor and responsibility, as well as other hidden problems. When one member of a couple is much more the O (organizer), he or she easily becomes like the parent of the D (distractor). Then you hear dialogues like this:

ELLEN (THE O): Honey, I was wondering if you've called Jimmy about the tax forms yet.

TOM (THE D): Didn't I tell you I'd do it?

ELLEN: Yes, but, sweetheart, you know you sometimes tell me you'll do things and then they don't get done. I'm just offering you a friendly reminder.

TOM: It doesn't feel friendly.

ELLEN: I'm sorry. How does it feel?

TOM: You know perfectly well how it feels. It feels exactly as you mean it to feel. Demeaning.

ELLEN: I don't mean it to feel demeaning. I just want the taxes to get done on time this year.

TOM: This year? See, you have to get in your little dig about how they didn't get done on time last year.

ELLEN: Or the year before, or the year before that, or the year before that.

TOM: And you say you're not demeaning?

ELLEN: I'm not trying to be demeaning. Truly, I am not. I'm just trying to figure out a way to help you get the taxes in on time.

TOM: No, you are trying to figure out a way, as usual, to exert your control over me and make me feel incompetent.

ELLEN: Tom, you are anything but incompetent. If you were incompetent, we wouldn't have all this income that we need to pay taxes on. It's just that you have this little problem around getting boring details organized. And sometimes those details can turn into big problems if you don't take care of them.

TOM: I wish I had a tape recorder. I really do. I wish I could play it back to you so you could see how you sound. You sound like you are talking to a ten-year-old about how important it is to get his homework in on time.

ELLEN: Honestly, Tom, sometimes that is exactly how I feel.

When one person fills the role of O, it is common for this kind of parent/child dynamic to develop. The longer the pattern continues, the more insidious it becomes. Ellen feels increasingly resentful, even as she does her best not to offend or talk down to Tom. Tom becomes more and more sensitive because he feels nagged and put-upon. Those feelings drive him to pull away from Ellen and ignore her urgings, which in turn makes Ellen feel more isolated and annoyed, less connected to her husband, and more burdened by her role as O.

A vicious cycle ensues. As Tom fails to follow through on details, Ellen feels compelled to remind him, which makes Tom resentful, and he avoids Ellen more. This, of course, makes Ellen feel even more disconnected, lonely, isolated, and resentful, while also more worried that the work that needs to get done isn't. All of these feelings drive her to pursue Tom ever more persistently and angrily. Tom begins to feel like a child being reprimanded, so he further avoids Ellen, which drives her to come after him even more tenaciously.

If the couple is not careful, their feelings for one another will significantly change. If one partner feels like a parent and the other partner feels like a child who's always done something wrong for which punishment awaits, this is not a recipe for romance. Quite the opposite. Romantic, erotic feelings dissipate. Lovemaking disappears. Anger and resentment crust the relationship and make the free flow of warmth all but impossible.

We have seen this many times in many couples. It is particularly difficult to fix when one or both parties dig in and refuse to listen to another point of view. The anger can run so deep, in the O or in the D or in both, that all each wants to do is hurl blame at the other. Fast-forward a year or so with Ellen and Tom and you might hear a dialogue like this:

ELLEN: Of course the taxes aren't done again. I'm so tired of you.

TOM: And how do you think I feel? All I ever get from you anymore is criticism. You're one angry woman, Ellen.

ELLEN: And you're one big baby, Tom. You think I like waiting on you hand and foot? You think I like having to bite my tongue every day because I don't want the children to hear what I really feel? Why can't you ever take responsibility? You don't get things done, then I remind you to get things done, and then you artfully make it sound like it's my problem because I nag you. You're clever, I'll give you that.

TOM: And you're a bitch, I'll give you that.

ELLEN: Oh, that's mature, Tom. But what can I expect from a man who won't grow up?

TOM: That's really helpful, Ellen. Just what every man needs to hear from his wife.

ELLEN: Believe me, Tom, you are not like every man.

TOM: Oh, and you want me to be Joe Ordinary like your fatuous brother you always want me to emulate?

ELLEN: He's not fatuous. And he is responsible. Yes, I wouldn't mind it if you were a little bit like that.

TOM: Then why don't you go marry him?

As you can see, this couple is stuck in the big struggle. They do little now but hurt each other's feelings. Without some kind of fresh insight or intervention, they could spend years simply tormenting each other or split up in a rancorous divorce.

The way out is through empathy. Whether it comes through couples therapy or simply through conversations between the couple, the anger needs to be set aside long enough for each person to understand the other's experience and to see through the other's eyes.

Self-justification must yield to empathic inquiry. Here is an example of each.

Self-justification:

ELLEN: I nag you because you never get anything done unless I do.

TOM: I don't get things done because you are always nagging me and I feel so resentful.

Empathic inquiry:

ELLEN: What makes it so difficult for you to organize the taxes on time? I'd really like to understand so I can help.

TOM: What is it that worries you so much about the taxes? I always get it done one way or the other. What upsets you so much about my putting it off? I'd really like to understand.

You need to add phrases like *I'd really like to understand* because when you start this approach, it will feel so new and different that your partner might suspect you are being sarcastic or avoidant.

But, once you make it clear that you do truly want to understand what is going on in the mind and the heart of the other person, then the other person can begin to explain.

But, beware. Some people, especially men, have the devil of a time looking into themselves and explaining what they feel or why they do what they do. Often, the most honest answer a person can give is "I don't know what's going on inside of me. I don't know why I feel what I feel. I don't know why I do what I do." In that case it helps if the other person can prime the pump, so to speak, by making some guesses. Empathy often begins in guessing. In fact, one way to define empathy would be as your best guess as to what another person is feeling or thinking. An empathic inquiry is really like the game of Twenty Questions as you zero in on what's going on inside the other person.

Let's say Tom is the one having a hard time explaining himself. The empathic inquiry could go like this:

ELLEN: I'm genuinely curious, Tom. Why do you put off the taxes when you know it will only create more problems?

TOM: I honestly don't know. The obvious answer is that gathering up all those documents is tedious and boring. But I can do other tedious and boring tasks.

ELLEN: Could it be that money makes you anxious? Or paying taxes makes you anxious? Or angry? And so you want to avoid it?

TOM: It certainly does make me angry. When I see how the government wastes the money, it makes me really angry, as you know. Do you think that could have something to do with it?

ELLEN: It could. Especially when you combine that with how laborious it is. Maybe a plan would be to have an expert we could hire come up with a system so you could basically do what you need to do every week, then there'd be no big crisis every April?

In this way the couple can work their way back from the parent/child alienating struggle and reestablish the kind of adult dialogue they both so want and need.

It takes forbearance, patience, and resolve to do this kind of work. If you can't do it alone, then consult a therapist. Just don't waste years in pointless and harmful struggle.

Sometimes the struggle can be resolved by spending some time simply dividing the chores that have to be done in a way that feels fair to each member of the couple.

Typically, couples like Tom and Ellen reach one of two solutions, both undesirable. They either let the O do all the work, or they fight about the division of labor every day and get nowhere except into the big struggle.

The seemingly mundane problem of who does what soon represents much larger issues. Who is in charge? Where is respect? Whose time is more important? Why can my voice not be heard?

Pretty soon, if you're not careful, the struggle takes a diabolical turn toward the blame game, full of accusations masquerading as psychological interpretations. "You expect to be waited on because your mother waited on your father." "You expect me to take care of you because when you were a little girl your father was never there for you and you're still trying to get him to prove his love to you." "You're so narcissistic you think the whole world revolves around you." "Your mother trained you to be a little prince who'd never lift a finger." "You have no power and control at work so when you come home, you try to exert power and control over all of us." "You know I am naturally a caretaker and generous and so you take advantage of that by letting me do all the work."

The underlying issues are always interesting; that's why just about everyone is an armchair psychologist. But often the discussion of these issues between members of a couple becomes just a sophisticated way of fighting. Progress doesn't get made and feelings get hurt.

Instead, we suggest you address the problem as follows. Acknowledge to one another that a lot of work needs to get done for the family to function. Acknowledge that each of you has different strengths and preferences, different tendencies and habits, and that none of these needs to be judged, but rather, simply, acknowledged.

Then, sit down together at the kitchen table with a pad of paper and an uninterrupted hour. Write down all the chores and responsibilities that have to be accounted for. Then, one by one, start volunteering for each of them. If neither of you volunteers for a certain item, skip it. Once you have gone through the whole list, go back to the skipped items and begin to haggle. Who likes this item least? Who is less equipped to take on this item? What would you do for me if I took charge of this item? Could one of the kids take on this item? Who else could do it? Whom might we hire or barter with (e.g., carpool) to get this chore done?

The session will likely take more than an hour, especially if you've been in the big struggle. It may take more than an hour just to get down on paper all the items that have to be divided up. But once you get the process started, you're on the road to a better place. You're on the road out of the big struggle.

If you find that you just can't do it without fighting, then it is worth hiring a referee, otherwise known as a therapist. One or two sessions with a good, practical-minded therapist can get you through your list on the road to recovery.

Once you have developed a division of labor that works, you'll be amazed at how much love you rediscover, how much energy you regain, and how much easier and more fun life becomes.

THIRTEEN

The New World of Affairs

People in committed relationships have been having extramarital affairs ever since the idea of a committed relationship first took hold. Humans are among the mere 3 percent of mammalian species, along with prairie voles, beavers, gibbons, and select others, who practice monogamy, or try to. While monogamy comes naturally via instinct to such animals as the prairie voles, we humans must contend with choice, temptation, guilt, memory, anticipation, and the other goodies that make us human. Instincts influence us, but they do not rule us.

Most of the issues involved in humans having affairs are anything but new. People have been falling out of love for as long as people have been falling in love. People have sought variety in their sex life for as long as people have been having sex. The allure of a tryst has long captivated people's imaginations, perhaps more than any other single step they might think of to spice up a dull life.

But what *is* entirely new in our age is the historically unparalleled availability of sex outside of marriage. Thanks to the Internet, anyone anywhere can go online and within seconds find a new partner. Short of a new partner, anyone can find more images of sex than one person could ever watch. Experts in the field of sex addiction explain that most people don't have even the remotest idea how widespread the phenomenon of sex online actually is—and how fast-growing it is.

Psychologists Patrick Carnes and Terrence Real, both of whom have years of experience in the field, caution that even most experts don't know the scope of the problem because it is so difficult to get reliable statistics. Carnes tells us that a "tsunami" of sex addiction is brewing due to the huge numbers of websites devoted to photos, video, chats, correspondence, and the setting up of rendezvous in person.

Short of a full-blown sex addiction, which we have not seen that often in our respective practices (in some cases perhaps simply because clients haven't told us their full story), we do hear with some regularity about a spouse having secret sessions on porn sites and even emailing strangers to have cybersex. "What's amazing is how careless they are. They almost always get busted, usually by their spouse," said Terrence Real.

What's going on out there? *Lots.*

First of all, ubiquitous, graphic, nonstop, 24/7/365 *temptation combined with instant access.* Cell phones, BlackBerrys, instant messaging, and texting provide instant availability. The kind of ready intimate exchange that email and texting allow—different even from speaking on the phone—is unprecedented. That, combined with all the opportunities the Internet affords, has created a whole new world of affairs.

No longer must one go out to bars in search of someone. No longer must one reply to personal ads or risk putting one's true identity on the line. Now it can all begin anonymously in private, from an office, a car, a hotel room, literally from anywhere, and the dialogue can instantly heat up.

Lacking the instincts of a prairie vole, how is the average human, especially the average man, to deal with this? For most men and for some women, making sex (images, chat, videos, as well as the easy chance to meet in person) so available in the privacy of an office or other place is tantamount to putting a naked member of the opposite sex in a nearby closet. It takes immense discipline never to open the door. Furthermore, many people see no reason they shouldn't open the door. It's legal. It's private. What's the harm? It's a safe way to get a thrill. Indeed, it can be argued that such availability is for the good. It allows people who might otherwise be visiting prostitutes to get the satisfaction they are seeking in a safer way. Perhaps. But the ease and speed with which impulse can turn into action, fantasy into reality, daydream into real-life encounter, is astounding. It's a slippery slope from one to the other.

Second, the new world of affairs provides instantly available focus. What do a roller-coaster ride, a horror movie, speed dating, a NASCAR race, ultimate fighting, and hooking up online have in common? They all focus the mind.

People are growing increasingly jaded to high stimulation. What used to be exciting or shocking is becoming banal. It takes an increasingly intense stimulus for people to feel engaged, focused, and fully alive. Ordinary life is just too boring. To get into the moment with full force, you need a jolt. Red Bull. Violence. Vertical skiing. Day-trading. An affair.

Often without being aware of it, most people are so scattered, juggling so much, being interrupted so often, that when they find themselves riveted, they love it. When we find some activity that so engrosses us that we forget who we are, where we are, and what we're doing, it feels sublime.

We can get into this highly pleasurable focused state in various ways. One of the best ways is to work on a challenging problem that interests you. Soon the activity engrosses you. You forget the time of day, you forget even if you're hungry, and you don't hear a knock on the door or the noises outside. Psychologist Mihaly Csikszentmihalyi named this state of hyperfocus "flow." He wrote an entire book about it, named, appropriately enough, *Flow*. Csikszentmihalyi's groundbreaking research showed that in the state of flow, humans are at their happiest as well as most productive. The more time we spend in flow, the better we do and the happier we are.

But it takes work to get into flow by tackling a problem and using your creative energies. However, a quick visit to a sex site takes no work and produces instant focus and flow.

Sex quickly leads to hyperfocus. Going online and looking at naked pictures can rivet a person's attention. Visiting a sex site can captivate the imagination. While this is not exactly what Csikszentmihalyi had in mind when he recommended flow, the mental focus that sex online can induce can be as captivating as flow—just not as useful.

Even more riveting than a sex site, though, is an actual, live interaction with a person you're not paying; in other words, an affair. The search here is not so much for sex, but for riveting connection. The person is not even aware of what he's looking for—but when he finds it, he can't get enough of it. This is why sex addiction is so on the rise.

Incidentally, the search for quick focus is a chief reason people visit gambling sites. Experts in gambling also talk about the tsunami Carnes described, citing the spike in problem gambling made possible by the Internet. Once again, the numbers are not known exactly, but all experts agree that the increase is beyond huge.

So, what to do about it? What to do about sex addiction, gambling addiction, the rapid rise in online affairs and real-life affairs? What to do when your spouse's computer becomes his plastic mistress?

Books are out now on how to detect the problem, how to snoop on your spouse's computer, and what signs to watch for that signal your spouse is having an affair. We're not interested in coaching you on how to become a cybercop, but we do have some suggestions on how to deal with the new world of temptation and availability, whether you are the spouse or the person caught up in one kind of liaison or another.

First, try to understand this new world and how it affects you. One of our patients said he doubted he would ever have had the many liaisons he had were it not for the availability of texting. Texting took on its own kind of erotic thrill. It was not the same as a conversation on the cell phone. It was more like interactive erotic literature. He said it provided a unique and quickly irresistible thrill, unlike anything he'd ever before experienced. He became an addict of erotic texting, which quickly led to a series of in-person encounters.

None of these encounters were emotionally laden. It was all about the sex, and he believed the women he was with felt the same way, as none of them asked him to leave his wife or anything like that. They were all hooked on the high stimulation they got from the texting followed by the in-person brief encounter.

He had never anticipated what a Pandora's box he was opening. By the time he understood, he had almost lost his marriage. Only through over a year of couples work and his having an understanding and loving wife was the marriage saved. Not for a minute had he stopped loving his wife. But he had fallen prey to a new kind of drug called, in his case, erotic texting.

You may judge this man harshly, but judgment is not what matters here. What matters is understanding that this new world brings with it new temptations.

Just as you know your limit when it comes to drinking alcohol, you need to know your limit when it comes to erotic activities of any kind online and what they can lead to off-line. Then plan accordingly what fits you and your relationship, from abstinence to anything goes.

Second, be clear with your mate about what is okay with each of you and what isn't. It is not up to us to tell you what is right or wrong, but we do urge you to decide together what you deem acceptable behavior and what you deem unacceptable. If you both want to have an open marriage, fine. If you both believe that visiting any erotic site online is fine or is forbidden, okay. Just make sure what's fine for one of you is fine for the other. Discuss the issue and get on the same page before one of you discovers the other doing something that could jeopardize your relationship.

Third, if you are wrestling with these issues unsuccessfully—if you can't resist the temptations the Internet offers, for example, even though you want to resist, take the struggle seriously. Just the fact you are struggling should tell you that you are in a danger zone. If you are not struggling at all, but are spending a lot of time in secret on erotic sites, then consider that you might be in one of the most dangerous zones of all, the zone we call denial.

If you are struggling, or if you think you might be in denial, don't judge yourself from a moral perspective. All such judgment does is instill shame, which only drives you further into secrecy, thus making the problem worse.

Instead, either by yourself, or better still with the help of a professional, ask yourself the following questions:

1. Why am I engaging in this secret erotic activity?
2. Is there something missing in me or in my life that I am trying to replace?
3. Am I using this activity as an antidepressant, a stress reducer, or a self-esteem booster?
4. Am I using this activity to avoid looking at other troubling issues?
5. Have I stumbled into something without knowing what I was getting into?
6. Would I like to put an end to it?
7. Is there a constructive way I could deal with the issues I am using this activity to avoid dealing with?
8. If I gave up my online erotic activity or the affairs I am having, what pleasurable activity or activities could I replace that with?
9. Who is a safe person I could discuss all this with to develop a plan of action?
10. Even if I am able to stop what I'm doing, how can I deal with the shame and guilt I feel?

Usually, it's best if you can discuss these questions with someone else, so your answer to question number 9 is important. If you can't think of someone, start with your family doctor or best friend.

Most of the time the compulsive or addictive sexual behaviors the Internet facilitates come under the heading of what addiction specialist Edward Khantzian of Harvard calls self-medication. As such, they can be treated by switching to an actual medication, such as an antidepressant or antianxiety agent, or even better, a metaphorical medication, such as insight, renewed intimacy with your partner, or a creative outlet in which you can invest the energies you've been putting into online sex, such as physical exercise, or a twelve-step program.

The underlying principle of twelve-step programs is to replace the drug or activity of abuse with the "drug" of fellowship or, to use our term, connection. No program has succeeded better than twelve-step programs in treating addictions.

Whatever course you choose, it is crucial to take the problem seriously, but not shamefully, and put together a plan that will rescue you from hurting yourself and those you love due to understandable human temptation gone out of control.

FOURTEEN

Time for Sex

While modern life has made it far easier to have extramarital affairs (especially if you include sex online as meeting the definition of an extramarital affair), it has made sex between committed couples paradoxically more difficult. It is not that making love has become more difficult—in fact, technology and medicine have made it far less difficult for many people—it's just that modern life offers so many alternatives!

For the same reasons it is difficult to get a person's attention in general, it can be difficult to get a person's attention long enough to have sex. As mentioned before, one of our patients refers to her husband's computer as "his plastic mistress." Another told us she had to argue with her husband to get him to turn off his BlackBerry while they were having intercourse.

Those may seem like extreme examples, but many couples wish they made love more often—but can't explain why they don't. They joke and say, "Who has time?" Or, "By the time I'm in bed, I'm ready for one thing—sleep!"

When pressed, most couples in this situation will say they miss having more of a sex life. They will say they are still attracted to each other. They will say they still have sexual desire. They will say they find lovemaking satisfying when they get around to it. They also say they know it is good for their general physical and emotional health to make love (it really is!), and they know that of course it is good for their relationship in general to be close sexually. Yet they still make love less often than they'd like to.

When one is more distracted, more the D, then the problem can become even more difficult. Let's say Mary is the D in the relationship and Hank is the O. As they sip coffee at the end of a meal, having set aside the evening for a "date night" out at a restaurant, free from the kids and other interruptions, the dialogue might go:

MARY: This has been really nice tonight. I'm so glad you came up with this idea. How did you think of it?

HANK: You won't believe me, but I was reading some magazine in the dentist's office and the article was about relationships. The author suggested a date night.

MARY: You were reading a women's magazine?

HANK: It was what was left on the table. But don't sound so surprised. Men like relationships, too.

MARY: Sure, but they don't usually read about them in magazines. At least you don't.

Hank paused and looked down at his cup of coffee. He waited a few seconds before saying these next words.

HANK: You know, I still think you're a knockout.

MARY: Why, Hank, that's the nicest thing you've said to me in, I dunno, ten minutes.

HANK: Seriously, Mare, you're beautiful. I love your eyes. And, might I add, your butt is still phenomenal.

MARY: Why, Henry Thomas, I do believe you want something to happen tonight.

HANK: Every night, hon. Every night.

MARY: Really? That's sexy. You want me every night. How about every day?

HANK: Yes, yes, day and night. How about me? How often do you want me?

MARY: You're making me blush.

HANK: You're my wife and we've been married seventeen years. We have four kids. I can't make you blush.

MARY: Well, you just did. The fact is, Mr. Thomas, that I find you as attractive and sexy as the day we got married. In fact, more so. And, I might add, you have one great butt yourself.

HANK: Then why don't we have sex more often?

MARY: Oh, Hank, we do it as much as anybody else does in our shoes.

HANK: Do we really? I was asking Alex—

MARY: You didn't!

HANK: Sure I did. Why not? Anyway, he said he and Nancy do it two or three times a week.

MARY: I bet he was lying. Anyway, that's not much more often than us.

HANK: Sweetheart, are you kidding? Do you have any idea how often we make love?

MARY: Well, I haven't been keeping a record, if that's what you mean.

Hank paused again, formulating his thought.

HANK: When I saw you come out of the shower this morning, I watched you standing there. You took a little glance at yourself in the mirror, then started drying off, and I felt a pang inside. I thought you were so beautiful and graceful and I wanted you so much right then, but I knew if I said anything, you'd feel pressured and not really into it, and you'd say you really had to get the kids up and get them to school and you to work. So, I didn't say anything. I just lay there a few minutes and ached inside. Then I got up, gave you a pat on the butt, and got into the shower.

MARY: I remember the pat on the butt. That was nice.

HANK: But wouldn't more have been even nicer?

MARY: Don't I satisfy you?

HANK: This isn't about you or anything you don't do right. I know you're so sensitive to that, like you always think you've failed in some way. This isn't about you. It's about us. But while I'm on it, not only have you not failed, you are the most awesome, satisfying, perfect woman in the world. Please don't take what I'm saying personally. That's why I almost didn't bring it up, because I knew you'd feel like I was blaming you or you'd just feel inadequate. This is a two-way street, babe. It's us. You and me. We just don't make sex the priority it ought to be. Look, we're really lucky. We still turn each other on. We still want to do it. We still love each other.

MARY: How'd you know I'd take it personally?

HANK: How'd I know? Mary, I know you, remember? And I love you. I just want to make love to you more.

MARY: It is my fault. I'm too busy, too tired, too this, too that.

HANK: No, I won't let you do that. This is nobody's fault. And we can fix it. Hell, it's a dirty job, but somebody's gotta do it.

Mary, who was about to cry, started to laugh.

MARY: You mean it? You're not mad at me?

HANK: Mary, how could I possibly be mad at you? You married a boring old stiff like me and you give me more fun every day than I ever thought I'd ever have.

MARY: You're not a boring old stiff.

HANK: Yes, I am. And I know it. But because of you, I don't mind being who I am. Because of you, I'm a happy man.

MARY: Who just wants to get laid more often.

HANK: Bingo!

Mary and Hank are lucky, of course. But their conversation illustrates several issues that they can take care of if they want to.

First, most obviously, sex. They contend with *the* great undiagnosed sexual "dysfunction" of this era: infrequent lovemaking due to being too busy.

Simple problem, right? Not so simple. And if it doesn't get taken care of, it can lead to many more problems, stemming from feelings of isolation and disconnection.

Being too busy is a national, if not worldwide, epidemic. Throw into the equation that Mary is prone to distraction and the problem instantly gets worse. She freely admits that she has trouble making time for sex, and she feels bad about it. But she doesn't know what to do.

A less understanding husband than Hank would either blame her and make her feel worse, or become sullen and pout. These are the two major boneheaded ways people deal with conflict. They either attack or withdraw. Both tactics only make the conflict worse.

But Hank took a different approach. He brought up the problem in a private, intimate setting and took responsibility for his share of the issue. He also framed it lovingly.

The next step ought to be easy. But it probably won't be. The next step is simply for Hank and Mary to schedule lovemaking into their lives. It probably won't be easy because it takes work to change habits, schedules, and routines. But with Hank and Mary committing to a date night, perhaps they will be able to tackle the paradoxically "difficult" problem of sex.

The solution is to make time for what matters most, in this case, lovemaking. It may sound unromantic to schedule sex. In fact, it is quite romantic. Let's say you pick Tuesday night at 10 p.m. You both agree to get the kids into bed or otherwise engaged, then you show up naked in bed at ten. You see what happens next. You might just start laughing at how contrived it all is. But you agree to stay. You play together. Pretty soon you're making love.

If making time doesn't do the trick, then look deeper. Making love is often a barometer of each partner's emotional state. If you are making love less often than you'd like to, ask each other if something is wrong. One of you may be angry, one of you may be depressed, one of you may be worrying over some unspoken issue, one of you may feel overburdened—and therefore not in a giving frame of mind.

Try not to get defensive as you have this conversation. No one is to blame. Feelings are just feelings. Don't let this discussion become a struggle. Instead, let it be an open-ended airing of feelings, a chance to understand what the other is going through emotionally. Often, as you explore such feelings, both of you will feel closer and will want to make love more often.

If such discussions lead nowhere, then try simply being more appreciative of one another. The discussions may fail because one of you isn't ready to speak, or one of you is not in touch with what he or she is feeling. If you can both resolve to be more appreciative of each other, even if it feels a bit forced, you'll likely find that you start to feel more relaxed, closer, and more cuddly with one another. You can't expect the problem to get solved in a day or two, but after a week or so you ought to see some progress.

If still one or both are feeling distant and not in the mood to make love, use the thirty-day workbook at the end of this book. The workbook gives you specific exercises to do, thirty minutes each day over thirty days, that are all but guaranteed to bring you closer to one another.

FIFTEEN

Just How Neat Must a Person Be?

Clutter is one of the most obvious defining characteristics of modern life. To us, it is perhaps best symbolized by the weed that was imported from Southeast Asia decades ago as a ground cover and became the scourge of Atlanta: kudzu. Once kudzu appears, it is all but impossible to eradicate. It has a nasty pinkish red root, sometimes as much as a hundred feet long. It spreads rapidly and can take over acres in no time.

Clutter is spreading like kudzu. Garbage has become the subject of an important science. We are gradually running out of space for our refuse. That's a global problem.

The local problem may be your desk. Or your basement. Or attic. Or kitchen drawers. Or living room. Or entire house.

Clutter is a by-product of our distracted age. If you are married to distraction, it is likely that you are also married to clutter: piles, messes, disorganized rooms, backyards, garages, basements, and attics.

One of the first casualties of distraction and overload is organization and neatness.

Neatness comes up far more often than it ever used to in the therapies we do with couples. Most couples seem to contend with how their house is organized or how their kitchen looks. Sue lives in fear of the mythical "visitors" who will unexpectedly arrive and pass judgment upon the appearance of our various rooms. These visitors have never come, but Sue believes in them as much as she believes in death and taxes.

So I often ask her, "How neat do we have to be to pass inspection?"

Her reply is usually incoherent, a kind of sputter of half-phrases and sounds of panic. The mere mention of a possible inspection sends her around the bend.

Some of this is her problem, but we both know she is far from alone. For generations, people, especially women, have lived in fear of their house being inspected and found wanting. What's different today is that there is so much more to straighten up.

One day, Ned called a junk-removal company and had half a truckload of "stuff" removed from our house. As the truck drove away, we could almost feel the house itself heave a sigh of relief. We all felt lighter, freer, less weighed down.

So it isn't only Sue who suffers due to the clutter and all the miscellaneous junk that fills the nooks and crannies, not to mention the tables and chairs, of our house. How many loads of old clothes do we take every year to Goodwill? Many. How many pens, baseball caps, scraps of paper, hangers, bottle caps, and rubber bands can appear on the floor minutes after it's been vacuumed?

Our house has a clutter generator. Ned may be the chief driver of it because he buys more unnecessary stuff than the four others who live here put together. Juicers. We now have four of them. They went away in the junk truck. Books. We buy them the way some people buy staples or paper clips. And presents for our kids? It's embarrassing to write it all down.

So we live with a constant influx of treasures and potential clutter. The question of neatness hovers over all of us.

Here's how I, Ned, resolve that question, and how I try to persuade Sue to resolve it.

I have given up on being neat as a pin. I have given up on the hope that all the socks in my drawer will match, or that I will know where all my sweaters are, or that my desk will look like the desks on the covers of business-furniture magazines. I have given up on the hope that the inside of my car will look like the inside of a rented limo, or that my wallet will not bulge with scraps of paper and bank receipts, or that the receipts will ever find their proper destination.

My ruling principle has become far more pragmatic, not to mention attainable. It is this: *do not let disorganization keep you from reaching your goals in life.*

Of course, a second guiding principle is needed: *don't choose crazy goals in life.* For example, I think trying always to be ready to pass a mythical house inspection is a crazy goal. Sue and I continue to go back and forth on this. To give another example, grading your parenting skills on the neatness of your teenager's room is a crazy standard. Or another example: trying to keep your house as neat as little Ms. Perfect's house down the street is a crazy goal. Try to rid yourself as much as possible of what William Blake called "mind-forged manacles." These manacles, which you create, can ruin an otherwise joyful life.

But you must be well enough organized that disorganization doesn't keep you from achieving your (sane) goals. You need to get to the job interview on time, you need to have clean dishes to eat from, you need to remember your spouse's birthday, you need to have *some* socks in your sock drawer, you need to keep track of how fast you're driving and when to turn right, and you need to know what day it is, but only if knowing what day it is matters in your achieving a goal.

Try to free yourself from what you imagine to be society's standards of neatness. Take charge of your own life, in cooperation with your spouse and children. Fire the house inspector. Laugh privately at little Ms. Perfect, who probably hasn't enjoyed a spontaneous moment in years. Look at your various messes and piles of clutter and smile. Look at them as evidence that you don't spend too much time doing what doesn't matter much after all. But don't let arguments over neatness take over your marriage as much as clutter can. Try to find the compromise, the happy medium.

SIXTEEN

Managing Anger and Frustration

He that is slow to anger is better than the mighty; and he that ruleth his spirit than he that taketh a city.

—THE BOOK OF PROVERBS

Anger is nothing new, and people who have problems with anger management have been with us forever. However, our age of distraction and overload is particularly apt to lead to problems with anger because a person is more likely to feel frustration and lose his temper when he is dealing with more than he is able to deal with in the time given for it.

Furthermore, when you can't get a person's attention, particularly your spouse's, your customary last resort is to yell and to get angry, which often begets an equally angry response.

Such anger can be tame, but sometimes it can be dangerous.

"I'm afraid of you," Gwen says to her husband, Pete. "I'm afraid to tell you I'm afraid, that's how afraid I am."

"Are you serious?" Pete asks. They're sitting at the kitchen table after dinner. The kids are downstairs in the basement watching TV.

"I'm very serious," Gwen says. "The way you exploded at dinner, it was unnatural. It was like so far out of proportion. You blew up because Bobby made a fart noise. Do you know how normal it is for a boy his age to do that?"

"But I want him to learn manners. Do you know how important that is?" Pete asks in a snarling tone.

"See? You're starting to rev up right now. It scares me."

"I can't believe you're serious. I've never hit you, I've never hit the kids, I've never even punched a wall or kicked the cat!"

"Pete, you have no idea what you're like when you get angry. We all freeze. Thank God you've never hit us, but your words hit really hard. I'm telling you this because I love you. Please don't get mad at me."

"For God's sake, Gwen, I'm not gonna get mad."

"Can you hear yourself, Pete?"

Pete, a short, wiry man, picks up a fork and squeezes it. "You're telling me you're afraid of me?"

"Yes, I am. The kids are, too. You don't want them to grow up afraid of you like you did with your father, do you?"

"I had good reason to be afraid of him. He beat the crap out of us every other day."

"I know, sweetie, I know. He was a terror. I know. But I have to bring this up. You are a kind man. You're not like your father at all. You just have to get a handle on your temper."

Rage is rampant in today's world. Due to many of the factors we've already named—speed, overload, pressure, insecurity, disconnection—most people live with higher levels of frustration and anger than is good for them. And they lack the usual healthy modifiers of their anger, such as exercise, friendship, sleep, and stability.

If anger is a problem in your relationship, don't ignore it, hoping it will go away. Uncontrolled anger kills respect. It instills fear. It prevents honest communication. It leads to abuse. It kills love.

The solution resides in the tools we have stressed throughout: attention, time, empathy, understanding. You may want to involve a therapist if one of you feels unsafe in discussing the issues with the other person openly and honestly. Do whatever you need to do to set up conditions for safe, ongoing discussions.

Once you have created the forum, a time and a place where you both feel safe, then bring up the issues. People's anger problems originate in a variety of ways. Many angry adults were abused as children. Many abusive spouses saw one of their parents abused. In a tragic irony, people tend to do to others what was done to them.

But being abused as a child or witnessing abuse are only two of many ways an adult can develop a problem with anger. Another common cause is the abuse of alcohol or other drugs. Drugs disinhibit a person and let loose pent-up anger and frustration. The term *an angry drunk* is well known because angry drunks are so common.

If childhood trauma or a drug or alcohol problem is causing the anger outbursts, then we strongly advise professional help. Trying to work it out without professional help can endanger the entire family.

But anger has many less serious causes. Simply the pressures of modern life drive millions of people to inappropriate outbursts of anger. The pace and demands of modern life tend to drive a person to anger often.

To be overly but necessarily simplistic for a moment, there are two states of mind. One, the good state, we call C-state. The adjectives that describe it begin with the letter *c:* cool, calm, collected, careful, convivial, curious, caring, concentrated, communicative, carefree, and consistent. The other state, the bad state, we call F-state. The adjectives that describe it begin with the letter *f:* fearful, frantic, frenzied, frustrated, forgetful, feckless; furious, and about to utter another F-word.

Modern life drives most of us into F-state now and then. Some people live in F-state most of the time. These people tend to have big problems with anger.

The key here is to learn how to identify F-state as it comes on, then to have a set of steps to follow to get out of F-state and back into C-state.

Take this seriously. Anger, more than any other emotion, ruins relationships.

Getting out of F-state takes only minutes, as long as you catch it in time. An excellent way to break F-state is a quick burst of exercise. Run in place vigorously or run up and down stairs a few times. Do twenty-five jumping jacks hard, or drop to the floor and do twenty-five push-ups. Whatever you do, a quick burst of physical exercise will dramatically change your brain chemistry. It is like pushing the reset button on your brain. You'll be back in C-state fast.

Another way is to divert your attention. Ned keeps a joke book in his desk drawer for F-state moments. Or, you can divert your attention simply by looking out the window and taking a few deep breaths.

Five minutes of meditation will break F-state. So will prayer. Calling a friend on the phone and talking about something completely removed from the problem at hand will usually restore C-state.

Then there is preventive maintenance. It is best to care for yourself in such a way that you minimize the likelihood of C-state. Get enough sleep (for most adults, seven to nine hours). Eat properly, avoiding junk food and fad diets. Don't self-medicate with drugs and alcohol. Exercise regularly. Practice meditation, yoga, or pray daily.

Furthermore, learn to construct boundaries around your time so that you don't constantly get interrupted. Learn to say no so that you don't overcommit. Don't waste time mindlessly screensucking with your electronic devices.

And *do* spend time with people you like working on projects you like. Try to arrange your work life so that you do something you're good at that you like, so you don't bring F-state home with you.

———

Beyond the various causes of anger—and their remedies—mentioned so far, we all have our own particular hot buttons. Here discussion, empathy, and understanding are key. Only by knowing your partner's hot buttons can you avoid pushing them. Only by understanding the source of those hot buttons can you feel for the person's plight.

Just as we each have particular activities that bring us pleasure, we all have particular activities or scenes that set us off. The more you and your partner can understand each other's, the better able you'll both be to help each other deal with the anger when it comes up.

Of course, not all anger is bad. More than two thousand years ago the Roman playwright Terence wrote, *Amantium irae amoris integratio est*, which means "Lovers' quarrels are the renewal of love." It is important to be able to get angry, as a means of sticking up for yourself. But anger should be like a sneeze. It should clear the air. But it should not last long. Anger that lasts a long time pollutes the air.

That leads to the final point in this chapter, which is the importance of forgiveness. Couples must know how to forgive one another if they are to thrive. We discussed forgiveness in the chapter on struggle stoppers, but mention it here again because it is such a necessary antidote to anger.

Remember, forgiveness does not mean, in our definition, that you condone the bad deed that was done or that you turn the other cheek. Forgiveness simply means that you get past anger and resentment. Not only is doing that good for your life as a couple, it is good for you as a person. Forgiveness is, in many ways, a gift you give yourself.

Do whatever you need to do to get past extended periods of anger. Of course, do not be a doormat. Stick up for yourself, but learn to forgive. You can learn to get past anger and resentment while at the same time preserving your safety and integrity.

Part 3

PROMOTING PASSIONATE
CONNECTION

SEVENTEEN

Conation: An Unfamiliar Key to Empathy

Chances are that you've never heard of the word *conation*. Yet this word could save your marriage or make your marriage stronger, less conflicted, and more fun. (The word could also save or strengthen your business, but that is for another book.)

Conation is the most powerful concept in psychology that nobody's heard of. We learned about it from Kathy Kolbe, the brilliant daughter of one of America's most accomplished psychologists, E. F. Wonderlic. Kathy has been studying conation for most of her adult life. She has developed a test by which a person can assess his or her conative style. Half a million people have taken the test, so the results, in the testing parlance, are well normed and validated.

What does *conation* mean and how can understanding it save marriages? *Conation* derives from the Latin word "to try." Your conative style is your style of trying. You've probably never thought about your style of trying; we hadn't until we met Kathy Kolbe. It had never dawned on us that either of us or anyone else even had a style of trying. But we all do, and it is valuable to know what yours is. Your spouse's, too. It is inborn, genetic, immutable, and persistent. You are born with your conative style and you die with it.

While we don't usually think of a person's style of trying, if you take a moment and reflect on the idea, you'll see what perfect sense it makes. Ned's style of making scrambled eggs is totally different from Sue's. Our respective style of taking a shower is quite different as well. When the undertaking grows more complex, knowing about your conative style can help you both understand why you do something the way you do it, and why others (such as your spouse) do it the way they do.

Given a river that you need to cross, for example, you might try to build a bridge, while one of us might try to swim it. You might seek help from an expert, while someone else might pray. You might consult a map, while someone else might build a raft. You might study all the possibilities, while your brother or sister or child might focus on just one. No single way is the right way of trying to cross the river. The ways of trying that each of us selects reflects our own, individual conative style, or what Kathy calls our modus operandi, our MO.

Your conative style or your MO refers to your natural, instinctive way of tackling a problem, managing a project, initiating an activity . . . or getting emotionally close to a human being. Also crucial, of course, are your cognitive style (your style of thinking) and your emotional or affective style (your style of feeling). But while most people are familiar with the concepts of cognitive and emotional styles, most people know nothing of the third element in the equation, the conative style, your instinctive way of *trying* anything.

Your conative style emerges once you move past thinking and feeling and commit your mental energy to a plan of action. Conation is *how you naturally and instinctively try to do something before anyone has told you what to do or how to do it.*

Think of your spouse. Let's say you are a woman and your spouse is a man. Let's say you've just asked him to fix the lawn mower. His conative style will be revealed by *how* he tackles the problem (cognitive and emotional issues will determine when and if he tackles the problem).

If he reaches for the owner's manual and starts to read it, that is one kind of conative style. If he walks out to the backyard and starts to tinker with the lawn mower, that is another conative style. If he calls a friend and asks for advice, that is another style. If he calls a repair shop and asks someone to come pick up the lawn mower, that is still another style. If he buys a new lawn mower or sells the house so that there will no longer be a lawn to mow, that is yet another style!

As you get a feel for conation, you will get excited at what a powerful explainer of people it truly is.

Let's say you give a woman you know a pile of junk and ask her to make something out of it. What she does next reflects her conative style. She might ask you a series of questions like "Why should I do this?" "What kind of item do you want me to make?" "What will be done with what I make?" "Where did the materials come from?" "How do I know that they are all safe and legal?" "Will I get paid?" "Who owns the patent if I make something valuable?"

On the other hand, she might just jump right in and start putting the pieces of junk together, creating some contraption of her own imagining without any apparent planning or forethought.

Or, she might ask for help from other people and start to supervise them as the project progresses.

Yet again, she might begin by sorting all the junk into various categories, say, metal in one pile, and in others, textile, vegetable, mineral, and miscellaneous. Or she might categorize the junk by size or by relevance to a design she has in mind.

Yet another conative style might lead her to step back and study the pile of junk and the potential project before doing anything else.

Everything you do is influenced by your conative style. But until now, it is likely you haven't had a clue that there was such a thing as a conative style or that your MO made a big difference in how you get along with your mate.

So far, the examples we've used are concrete, from crossing a river to fixing a lawn mower to making something out of junk. But think of getting along with your spouse. Notice how easily issues arise that reflect a conative style, an MO. Let's say you are a man and your spouse is a woman. Let's say she looks at you and states, "I'm too fat." Your conative style or MO partially determines how you respond.

One MO would lead you to say, "No, you're not!" You jump right in and want to fix the problem.

Another MO would lead you to say, "What makes you think so? You didn't feel fat yesterday when you said how good you felt about yourself." You want to explore the issue and get more facts.

Another MO might lead you to say, "Come over here and let me hold you so I can show you how perfect you are." You take a hands-on approach.

None of these is "right." How you respond depends upon your MO.

Kathy Kolbe divides conation into four categories, or what she calls action modes. The first she calls Fact Finder. The second she calls Follow Thru. The next she calls Quick Start, and the final one she calls Implementor.

When you take the Kolbe quiz,* you will get a numerical score from 1 to 10 in each action mode. Ned's score, for example, is 5–2–9–3. What does your Kolbe profile tell you? It describes your MO.

People who get a high score in Fact Finder (from 7–10) tend to solve problems first by getting as much information as they can. They investigate. They gather data. The more information, the better. People who get a low score in Fact Finder (from 1–3) go on the gist of the situation. They get impatient with too much fact-finding. And people who score in the middle (4–6) can go either way: they can research if need be, or they can comfortably act on a limited supply of information. A 5 in Fact Finder makes Ned both able to gather all the information he needed to get through medical school and do the research needed to write books, but also allowed him to write the sixteen books he's written and not spend fifteen years writing just one book.

People who score high in Follow Thru oversee a project from beginning to end. Those who score low in Follow Thru are the delegators.

People who score high in Quick Start jump right in and start doing, even before they have assessed the situation completely. Those who score low in Quick Start assess the risks and benefits thoroughly before they take action.

People who score high in Implementor are the hands-on types, the

---

* To learn more, go to www.Kolbe.com and take the test.

builders, the ones who solve problems by tinkering. Those with a low score in Implementor visualize the building, but they do not build it.

Let's take a look at how this might play out in the world of relationships.

In introducing the idea of a D and an O earlier in the book, we were describing MOs. In Kathy Kolbe's vernacular, a D, a distractor, would tend to score high in Quick Start and low in Fact Finder and Follow Thru, while an O, an organizer, would tend to score low in Quick Start and high in Fact Finder and Follow Thru.

The reason that the D and the O distinctions, or Kathy Kolbe's more elaborate distinctions, can be so powerful in helping couples is that they can take you from the realm of "moral diagnoses" and the struggles those cause into the realm of valid psychological constructs that are value-free. You can go from struggle to empathy and understanding.

An example, let's say Donna's Kolbe score is like Ned's, 5–2–9–3. Let's say her husband Will's score is 9–7–2–8. Without an understanding of the Kolbe concepts, a typical interaction could go like this:

WILL: What shall we do this weekend?

DONNA: Let's see how we feel Saturday morning and decide then.

WILL: No, I want to have a plan. It will be better for the kids if they know what to expect, too.

DONNA: But I don't know now what I'll feel like then. And the kids can take it. They actually love surprises.

WILL: Not always.

DONNA: Okay, not always, but often. I don't keep count.

WILL: I do.

DONNA: I'm sure you do.

WILL: Why, you think that's bad? You think it's bad I keep track of things? Well, I don't particularly like your devil-may-care attitude. I like a little structure and discipline in my life."

DONNA: So what does that make me, an irresponsible free spirit?

WILL: You said it, not me.

DONNA: Do you really mean that? Do you know how freakin' boring this family would be if it weren't for my spontaneity and fun ideas?

WILL: So, you're calling me a stiff?

DONNA: You said it, not me.

And so it can go, tit for tat, insult for insult, attack and defend, misunderstanding heaped upon misunderstanding.

If, instead, Donna and Will understood each other's MO, they could avoid a struggle and have a constructive conversation. It might go like this:

WILL: What shall we do this weekend?

DONNA: Let's see how we feel Saturday morning and decide then.

WILL: That's my Donna. Always wanting to be spontaneous. Such a quick-start.

DONNA: I know you'd prefer to have a plan. I understand that. That's my Will for sure. And it is a good thing one of us can make plans!

WILL: How about if we make a plan now, but make it tentative, so that come Saturday morning, if we're in the mood for something different, we can change the plan without anybody feeling upset?

DONNA: That's why I love you, Will. You can even make a plan for how not to have to stick to a plan.

Using their understanding of each other's MO, they easily avoid a struggle and appreciate the other person's strength, while not having to give up their own preferred way.

EIGHTEEN

Special-ize

Happiness is not having what you want, but wanting what you have.

—ANON

To want what you have is to be happy in life. If you can learn to make the details of your life special to you, treasured by you, then you will be happy no matter how much or how little you have.

When you want what you have, then envious, invidious comparisons of your life to someone else's disappear, or at least don't matter as much. When you want what you have intently enough, then you have all you need, no matter how much or how little you have.

But life—especially media-rich modern life—forces envy and resentment upon us at every turn with its distracting barrage of all-but-impossible-to-attain images of wealth, power, and beauty. It is tough in today's world not to compare yourself to the fabulously wealthy athlete, CEO, or movie star because their stories are so public. It can be difficult to rejoice in what you have and feel fully satisfied when, after all, who are you and I? Just another guy or gal. In fact, the pro football coach Bill Parcells coined a disparaging term for who you and I are. We are JAGs. A JAG is just another guy. How can we relish who we are? We're JAGs, part of the vast army of the not-rich-and-famous. We're the ones who are living lives of quiet desperation, right? We're longing to be rich and famous, but, since we're not, we are left to mutter and stumble through our forgettable lives. Isn't that correct?

Not if we sufficiently want what we have. Furthermore, many of those CEOs, athletes, and movie stars are actually the ones living lives of desperation (usually not quiet). You may think it would be just fine to change places with one of them, but if you actually want what you have enough, you'd turn down the offer every time.

If you think you would change places with one of those big shots, let us try to talk you out of it. Let us introduce you to the art of making your own life special. You *can* learn how to do it. It is an art we have named *special-izing,* the art of making your life special enough that your life becomes enough to fulfill you. Part of doing it is learning how to special-ize your marriage.

If you let what's special drain out of your marriage, you're in trouble. In the movie *The Story of Us,* the character played by Michelle Pfeiffer tells how she gave her husband a plastic spoon for their first anniversary. This spoon was special because they had used it to eat their first bowl of wonton soup while in the park, and the husband was thrilled to receive it as an anniversary gift. But then, over time, as the couple drifted apart, that spoon began to lose its meaning. "I wonder," Michelle Pfeiffer's character says, "when it is in a marriage that a spoon becomes just a spoon."

You do not have to let an important spoon become just another spoon, like a JAG. It is all in how you look at the spoon . . . or how you look at yourself . . . or how you look at your marriage. This is the secret. This is why you don't need to be a CEO, movie star, or pro athlete to feel special. The specialness derives not from the spoon but from how you regard the spoon. Such a simple point, but it makes all the difference in the world. It gives you the power of making life magical, rather than hoping against hope that you'll win the lottery.

In all that we do, whoever we are, we can make whatever we do, wherever we are, matter so much to us that it becomes enough, enough to make us feel as if we were the CEO, star, or whatever other royalty we have in mind.

Of all the arts a person can master, the art of special-izing may be the most significant. It carries with it the power of lifelong joy.

It is a cliché that the special luster soon fades from a marriage. How long it takes, so conventional wisdom tells us, varies. Maybe a year, maybe seven, when you get that famous itch, or maybe ten. But it fades.

It fades for many reasons, most commonly the accumulation of pain, misunderstanding, and loneliness, combined with a gradual humdrumification of the relationship.

You can prevent this. Much of this book tells you how to deal with the accumulation of pain, misunderstanding, and loneliness. This chapter tells you how to prevent or reverse the humdrumification of the relationship. All it requires is that you learn how to special-ize.

Special-izing begins in childhood. Ned's grandparents taught him the art of special-izing:

I had only three grandparents, as my father's dad died before I was born. Their lessons in special-izing began in the names I called them. We often give our grandparents special names. In my case, I called my mother's parents Skipper and Gammy McKey, and I called my father's mother Gammy Hallowell.

Whenever I visited Skipper and Gammy McKey, they took an avid interest in me. It is not so much that they spoiled me, although I suppose they did, as that they spent special time with me. The time they gave me was not driven by an agenda. The only agenda was to have fun together.

We did ordinary activities with extraordinary energy. For example, I remember Skipper spending what felt to me like a long time teaching me how to shake hands. He told me to look the other person squarely in the eye and shake that person's hand as hard as I could. He turned this into a funny game by challenging me to shake harder and harder and look ever more intently into his eyes. Staring and shaking as hard as I could, I giggled and giggled as the game went on. To this day, people often remark on how forceful my handshake is!

Gammy McKey worked a different magic. She would always head

into the kitchen upon my arrival. I knew what was coming, which made it all the better. After a few moments, she would emerge with a plate heaped with pieces of homemade fudge. As she presented the plate to me, she would tell me I could have "one in each hand." Instead of politely taking just one piece, which I would be told to do at home, Gammy would let me take one piece for each hand! What luxury. To this day *one in each hand* is my shorthand for abundance.

I should add that Gammy McKey and Skipper were far from wealthy. They lived in a cottage and barely had enough money to get by. But they had enough money to teach the art of shaking hands, to make fudge, and to make every visit to their house special for me.

Gammy Hallowell, on the other hand, was wealthy. Part of what made visits to her so special were the trappings of her wealth: a vast house overlooking the ocean; a sailboat moored at her dock; a croquet court behind her rose gardens; the first color TV that I ever watched.

She expected a certain kind of behavior and attire—she was a grande dame, an old-fashioned aristocrat, living according to rules of old-fashioned formality—but she made rising to her expectations *fun.* It was fun to get dressed up, it was fun to have dinner with finger bowls, it was fun to see Gammy in her flowing gowns and the gentlemen guests in evening attire.

But the heart of what made visiting her so special did not depend on money or aristocracy. She devoted the same energy to me as Skipper and Gammy McKey. She wore a charm bracelet with the name of each of her eight grandchildren inscribed on a charm, and she treated us all like treasures. She invited us to snuggle in bed with her every morning, and I can remember her musky, pleasant smell as if it were yesterday. She allowed us to have our scrambled eggs made with cream, not milk; that was like her version of fudge.

As we grandchildren got older, she would tell us that she expected us to give back to the world in special ways, thus extending the specialness from what we received to what we could give. I did not experience her expectation of giving back as a demand but rather as a goal to which I enthusiastically aspired. To this day, the pleasure I take in my achievements is deeply flavored by Gammy expecting me to give back.

Whenever I visited any of my grandparents as a child, I felt as if I were entering into an enchanted kingdom. Even the last visit I had with Skipper, when he was dying of emphysema (he smoked all his life), he smiled up at me from the couch where he lay and said, "One last handshake, old boy!"

In the grip of a special-izer like Skipper, life zeroes in on the present moment and only that moment. The moment need not even be happy—that last moment with Skipper made me cry—but it is *enough*. It will be enough to fill you up. The great gift of special-izing is that it makes whatever you are doing all that you need or want to do just then. For the time it lasts, you want what you have.

A great problem people face in their lives these days is their inability to turn any moment into enough. They are tormented by an insatiable desire for *more:* in their marriage, their career, their wealth, in everything. If you can't learn how to special-ize, then you will never find lasting joy, you will always crave more, you will live in a constant search for the next fix.

Gammy McKey, Skipper, and Gammy Hallowell were such excellent special-izers partly because they were grandparents. Grandparents tend to be excellent special-izers because they do not have to keep their grandchildren full-time! They can make the visits so special because they are brief.

So, how do you special-ize a marriage? Unless your spouse travels a great deal, his or her "visits" home are not brief. Your spouse lives with you full-time. Is it possible to special-ize a full-time relationship?

It is, but with some important qualifications. You can't expect *every minute* to be special. You must allow for periods of boredom, conflict, even dislike. You must not look at every blowup as evidence that your marriage is on the rocks. You must accept that prolonged intimacy necessarily includes arguments, disagreements, periods of not liking the other person a whole lot, and feelings of being ignored, misunderstood, rejected, and exploited.

You've got to expect all of that and not let it throw you off stride.

So how then do you special-ize an intimate relationship, given all the obstacles that necessarily arise? You use the tools we emphasize throughout this book: attention sustained over time; empathy and understanding; connection; play.

In addition, you use a recipe that includes five ingredients:

1. Knowledge of what the other person wants and loves, and communication of what you want and love.
2. "Something extra."
3. Traditions and rituals.
4. Boundaries.
5. Investment of positive energy in the moment.

The first ingredient, knowledge of what each other wants and loves, is an outgrowth of empathy and connection. Gammy McKey knew that *Ned* loved fudge, and she knew that *she* loved to see a smile on his face. Put the two together and you get a special moment for each person.

So the first, simple, but often not completed step in special-izing your marriage is to take an inventory of what your spouse *really likes*.

This makes for an enjoyable conversation. What do you really like? Salted peanuts? Ice cream at midnight? Bob Marley? The crispy skin of a roast chicken? A manicure? Guilt-free football on TV? Going as a family to get the Christmas tree? Fresh-cut flowers? Pinot Grigio? Paris? Back rubs? Thanksgiving? *Meet the Press?* Fast cars? Golf? Breakfast in bed? A certain sexual act? An afternoon nap? Freshly squeezed orange juice? Whatever your personal pleasures, knowing what they are is phenomenally important for each spouse. Only if you know what the other person adores can you provide it. And only if your spouse knows what you adore can he or she provide that. Special-izing depends upon knowing what the other person wants.

———

The second ingredient, "something extra," defines special. If an experience is ordinary, then it isn't special. This is why not nearly every moment can be felt as special. Even the most devoutly spiritual person who feels that every second of life is a gift from God that should be treasured and celebrated gets bored now and then. It is impossible to make every second stand out as special. Only a minority of our seconds can make the grade. That's why we call them special.

Gammy McKey understood the importance of something extra when she allowed Ned a piece of fudge *in each hand*. The fudge itself was excellent, but what made the experience special was getting one piece in each hand.

So, don't feel bad if you can't always give the extra time, the extra helping, the extra day away, the extra whatever. Just know that when you can provide the something extra, you've likely made that moment special.

Take an extra second on the good-bye kiss. One time bring home a carful of roses, not just a bouquet. Give the back rub for thirty minutes instead of thirty seconds. Write a three-page letter instead of just a quick inscription on the birthday card. Add a bottle of champagne to dinner at home some night. Offer to take a walk and look at the sunset.

And maybe most important of all, give extra attention to details. Notice . . . *everything you can!* If you look closely at a patch of grass, maybe with a magnifying glass in hand, you'll find all manner of bits of dirt, critters, debris, shapes and shades of grass, and much more. If you look closely at any person walking down the street, you can write what you imagine to be his or her life story. If you look closely at the people you know, you can see much of what they can't even see for themselves. If you look closely at the details of life even at its most mundane, you can make life become more vivid—and special—than it used to be.

Whether you believe that or not, you can make another person feel special if you will take the time to notice the details of his or her life. The new haircut. The old dress that hasn't been worn in a while. The sad look. The eyes turned away. A chair placed differently in the living room. A necktie. The color of socks. A possible promotion. A neighbor's reaction. The smile that greets you. The tone of voice on the telephone.

Noticing details is the simplest and surest tool we've got to turn the ordinary into the special. The world puts forth a shimmer of ordinary shade, and behind that screen all the telling truth resides. The something extra you give when you notice a detail makes that moment instantly better than it had been. If you make it a habit to remark on details, your life will start to become more vivid in your eyes, as well as the eyes of your spouse.

It is not the lack of *more*—money, achievement, material goods, status—that renders so many lives inadequate and even desperate in the eyes of those who live them. It is the lack of attention to detail. It is the absence of notice taken by the individual and by others. People collude to turn what could be extraordinary into inadequate simply by not taking stock, by not noticing all that surrounds them.

Try not to take your spouse for granted. Try to notice what is there to be seen. Try to see him/her with fresh eyes every day. Of course, this is impossible to do all the time, but make the effort when you can. It is a favor you do yourself as well as your spouse. We are all starved to be recognized in our full details.

It is such a paradox: so many people starving in the midst of a feast. We all do it. We get caught up in the pursuit of what we want to such an extent that we overlook what we already have. But by doing this we risk diminishing, or even losing, what we have.

For example, if you don't relish, make special, notice, and enjoy your children while they are growing up, when they leave, you will have missed a great chance. And in your marriage, if you don't relish, make special, notice, and enjoy the little details every day, you risk those details disappearing.

———

The third ingredient in special-izing, traditions and rituals, may seem like a contradiction of "something extra." Isn't a tradition or ritual, by definition, the expected, usual, ordinary way of doing something? Yes. You might say that traditions and rituals are the flip side of something extra.

Traditions are rituals that give you something to look forward to. Even though you know what's coming, knowing what's coming is what makes it special. For example, in our family we have a tradition of opening presents Christmas morning followed by a breakfast of biscuits with sausage gravy. This recipe, which comes from Sue's childhood in Virginia, has become a cornerstone of our Christmases. If Sue didn't make sausage gravy and biscuits, we would all feel that Christmas lacked a special something. By making those biscuits and sausage gravy every year not only does Sue add some deliciously unhealthy food to our lives, she carries on a family tradition and helps make Christmas special.

These rituals need not be made special simply by being rare, such as once a year, at Christmas. We have a daily ritual, as do many families, of having dinner together in the evening. Each of us sits in the same seat. If someone is missing, that person's name gets mentioned in the blessing we say before the meal. We take note of everyone, including our dog, Ziggy. The specialness of family dinner accrues over time. We each look forward to it, and we each would hate to miss it, even though we often argue during dinner. It is not the pleasantness of the dinner that makes it special, it is the predictability, the reliability. It gives us a mooring in an unmoored world.

You can create rituals and traditions in your marriage to add to its specialness. Sue always puts flowers on the hallway table in our house, and this has become a kind of ritual for us. Because Ned has to leave the house early every Wednesday morning, Sue gets up for breakfast, even though she could easily sleep in. That's become a ritual, one we both love. I bring her breakfast in bed on certain days. We always kiss good-night.

Lovemaking usually includes a kind of routine. Often, sex experts encourage people to break these routines, and if you are bored with your sex life, you ought to break your routine. But routines in lovemaking can become enjoyable rituals, a predictable and satisfying way to give and receive pleasure. Don't feel bad if you like your predictable sex life. Predictable sex can be the best sex!

Traditions and rituals work their magic by combining anticipation with predictability. When you know that a good thing will happen, the anticipation of the good thing adds to its specialness. Birthdays, Valentine's Day, Mother's Day, Father's Day, the Fourth of July, Thanksgiving, all the holidays and other days of celebration give off their glow all year round because we know in advance that they *will* happen. Far from being the enemy of special, predictability can be its great friend.

Be creative. Think of rituals and traditions you can initiate with your spouse. The longer you practice them, the more special they'll become. A Thursday-night date night. One of you making breakfast for the kids Sunday morning. Showers together whenever it rains. Pink roses on Groundhog Day. Reading aloud to each other in bed. A new piece of lingerie or a special sexual favor whenever one of you has a special success at work. A walk together before breakfast. Lunch in the city on the third Wednesday of every month that has a *y* in it. Every year, a day called Sex and the City, when you spend a day and a night in the city, in a nice hotel, go shopping, to museums, a ball game, or all of these. Let your imagination go. Make up your own rituals and traditions.

——

The fourth ingredient, boundaries, is especially vital in today's world. Nothing can be special if it is constantly interrupted. You must be adamant about protecting special time, otherwise it will lose its power.

For example, family dinner quickly loses its specialness if you take phone calls during dinner or watch TV or allow people to send text messages while they eat. How many families squander their chance to create this special time at dinner simply because they do not insist on protecting that time?

The electronic devices are the great boundary violator. Lunch with a close friend can become far from special; it can become insulting if that friend takes calls and checks his email while you eat. Technology, our great servant, can become our great thief if we allow it to steal away our special moments.

Such "conveniences" can create madness and portend the end of a relationship if we do not erect boundaries of our own choosing to replace the boundaries space and time used to impose. Today, as never before in human history, constructing boundaries is essential for doing just about anything well, which certainly includes maintaining a passionate relationship.

Nature used to do the job for us. Now that we have broken down most of the barriers nature used to impose, we must resist our temptation to become addicted to our electronics, lest we let them replace our intimate relationships.

Without boundaries, no intimate encounter can become special.

——

The fifth ingredient in our receipe for special-izing your marriage, positive energy, requires that you summon up your emotional reserves, even if you're not in the mood. That may sound laborious. You may think that to be special a moment ought to be spontaneous and require no "summoning" of any kind. Sometimes it happens, but special moments will happen more often if you work at it a bit.

While some special moments will come as naturally as leaves to a tree, if it is winter, and there are no leaves, you don't want to have to wait until spring! If you are not getting along, you don't want to have to wait it out to make things special again. Try digging deep. Try finding the positive energy that does reside inside of you somewhere, then use it to break the ice.

No moment nor any event can rise to the level of being special without the infusion of extra energy, positive energy. When this doesn't arise spontaneously, pump it in. Your pumping it in will tend to bring it out of the other person, sooner or later.

Often couples fall into the habit of taking each other for granted, of simply doing what has to be done, reacting to one another, and getting on, so that life becomes quite humdrum. You can change this in a heartbeat simply by putting forth some warm and loving energy. This doesn't necessarily have to be sexual energy, but rather, the energy it takes to value another person intently, to value being together intently, to connect in a positive way.

—

When you do what it takes—and our recipe is just one version of what it takes—to special-ize your marriage, then no problem matters as much as it used to. You are happy with each other, and the world can go its way.

NINETEEN

Building Romance

The question of how to keep romance alive, or regain it once it has disappeared, has filled thousands of books, not to mention magazines. For our purposes in this book, the question becomes, how do you keep your romance alive if you're married to distraction?

Romance, which includes sex but much more as well, depends upon many qualities, such as allure, mystery, intrigue, suspense, playfulness, naughtiness, abandon, trust, imagination, and creativity. But above all, it depends upon focus. It depends upon attention. Without attention, there can be no romance. There can be sex, albeit not very satisfying sex, with minimal attention, but there can be no romance.

So, before you go to the lingerie store, the sex-toy store, or the newsstand to buy *Cosmo*, make a date. Set aside a time to be with your mate. Go for a drive. Go out for a walk. Go to where you went on your first date. Get to know each other again in a setting that allows, first and foremost, for attention. Create a scene in which the cell phones get turned off and the chance for an interruption sinks to slim or none.

Then, sit next to each other, or across from each other, or walk hand in hand, or sit in the car as one of you drives, play music you both like, and talk about . . . whatever. The conversation might go like this:

"Do you remember the first time I asked you out?"

"Yes, I turned you down."

"Yes, you did. You said I was too much of a womanizer, which was totally unfair and untrue!"

"It was totally true! And my turning you down is probably why we ended up getting married."

"You're right. It got my attention, that's for sure."

"It's nice to have your attention now. It isn't easy to get."

"Yes, this is nice. You're right. I'm always on the go, aren't I? Too busy. You're right. I should listen to you more. I don't often get a chance to tell you how much I love you."

"Do you?"

"What?"

"Love me?"

"Do you doubt it?"

"I guess not. But I like to hear it. If I don't hear it, then I start to doubt it. Isn't that like a rule of nature? Love must be stated or it gets doubted. I think Isaac Newton meant to include that in his laws."

"How often must it be stated? After all, I do tell you now and then."

"Now and then is probably not optimal. Every ten minutes would be good. But I could settle for every day."

"I've fallen a bit short of that."

"Just a bit. It's in your self-interest to do it, you know. That is, if you want those special favors you seem to so enjoy."

"Yes, I do enjoy them. And, I might add, you seem to enjoy them yourself."

"But I would never admit to such a thing! What do you take me for?"

"Oh, just some girl I know. And love."

———

In just a few lines, in just a few moments, romance can get a quick kick start between two people who once had it. If you once had it, and most couples did, you can get it back. Tap into memory. Take a detour around hurt and anger. Play. And above all, pay attention.

Set aside time to linger with each other but have no agenda. We often "prescribe" for our patients a weekly date night. If your schedule won't allow that, make it a biweekly or monthly date night. If your schedule won't allow even that, run, don't walk, to a good couples therapist—or work the workbook at the end of this book.

You do need to make the time, one way or another. Find your own way. Maybe it's ten minutes in the evening, or an hour on Sunday morning. Maybe you go for a walk together before breakfast, or maybe you have a pillow fight at midnight. Maybe you buy cans of whipped cream and spray each other while standing in the shower. Or maybe you do something even sillier than that. The sillier the better. Silly is fun. Fun is good.

However you do it, find time to pay undivided attention to each other with no agenda of any kind, other than to connect and enjoy being together.

You do *not* have to talk about weighty matters. In fact, it is probably better that you don't. Who needs another argument? Be spontaneous, be frivolous, be playful, chitchat about stupid, little things. Romance thrives on small talk about stupid, little things.

In such a setting, you will start to play. And as we stated at the start of the book, play is the action of love.

One of our personal silly, little games is to make rhymes. One of us will say something, the other will rhyme it, and back and forth we go. The "winner" is the one who makes the last rhyme. Such a "conversation" might go like this:

"I'm going to bed."

"Okay, Fred."

"My name is Ned."

"The man I wed."

"Until I'm dead."

"Or find someone else instead?"

"What put that thought in your head?"

"You're turning red!"

"I like brown bread."

"That's bread I dread."

About now one of us runs out of quick rhymes and the other declares him/herself the winner. It makes us both laugh. It is silly, but we always have fun with it. Silliness is a great de-stressor.

It is good to find the little playful rituals, zones you can enter where all your cares disappear, and for a few minutes you are simply like kids on a playground, having fun together, while the rest of the world works its serious way around the sun.

It is good to do this often and regularly. Just one date night won't help much. Most people who take our advice but have just one date often spend the evening arguing and end up feeling worse than ever.

Instead, the idea is to reserve "special time" for each other regularly. Twenty minutes a week can do the trick, as long as it is every week. The only ground rule is that neither of you allows any interruptions during those twenty minutes, and you agree not to discuss matters of conflict. Basically, you are agreeing to have fun together— which may not at first be as easy as it sounds, but will become easier the more you do it.

Look at all the activities you do make time for. Surely, you can make time for your number one person, just twenty minutes each week. If you do this regularly and abide by the simple ground rules, within weeks you will start to notice a positive change, and within months you will feel closer to each other than you have in a long while. It beats zoning out in front of the TV or online.

The final section of this book is a workbook in which we set out a plan for you to spend thirty minutes together each day for thirty days. We call those thirty minutes "present time" because the only requirement is that you be entirely present during that time. If you follow the workbook, your relationship can't help but deepen and grow.

TWENTY

The Unexpected Gift

Before we meet, we're alone. Each of us deals with being alone in different ways. When we marry—or enter a long-term relationship—our "aloneness" changes, often in surprising ways.

We have a friend who hates being alone. Whenever she is alone, she gets anxious. She worries she is being excluded by some group or individual. She panics or gets sad or both. Even though she "knows" she is wrong in imagining she is being excluded, she nevertheless feels in her heart that she is being rejected by someone whenever she is alone. Therefore, she does her best never to be alone. She surrounds herself with people almost every waking minute in her life.

We have another friend who loves being alone. She relishes the freedom to do whatever she wants without having to please someone else or make compromises. She finds the company of other people tolerable, but not nearly as fulfilling as being alone.

Both of these people are married. We think of them as opposite ends of a spectrum. Most of us fall somewhere in between on the aloneness spectrum. We like our alone time up to a point, but we also like being with others.

When you marry or enter some other long-term relationship, you learn how to manage both your style of being alone as well as your partner's style. They may conflict, but you try to work out a deal that allows each of you to be true to yourself.

Our busy, distracted modern world, full of distraction and overload, makes being alone more difficult now than ever. It is, of course, easier than ever for the friend who hates being alone to find connections, however superficial. It leads our friend who loves her solitude to construct unusually strict boundaries. For example, she does not use email, and she often does not answer her telephone. This has some negative social repercussions, but she doesn't care. She sometimes wants people to leave her alone.

We all have an "alone self." When you think of yourself alone, you conjure up a set of feelings and see yourself engaging in a characteristic repertoire of activities.

For me, Ned, the alone self is full of sorrow. Because I was often lonely as a child, was party to much traumatic conflict at home, and was sent away to boarding school at the age of ten, being alone even now triggers feelings of sadness from youth. As an adult who travels a lot, I have to be alone in hotel rooms often. There, my repertoire of activites is often geared at staving off sadness. My strategies are simple. I phone home. I order room service. I watch television.

Our friend who loves being alone has an alone self quite different from Ned's. When she thinks of herself being alone, she glows. Her repertoire of alone activities is far richer than Ned's in hotel rooms. She bakes bread and cooks elaborate meals for her family. She digs in her garden, which she loves as if it were her child. She walks the family dog. She reads. Does she ever read! Two or three books a week. Her alone self is almost always engaged in some creative or active outlet.

It is good to know your alone self and, if you can, develop it as fully as our friend who loves being alone has developed hers. Some people believe that your alone self is your "true self," but we disagree. It is simply the self that emerges when you are alone. It is no more or less true than the self you become when you are with other people. But it is usually different from your social self, sometimes slightly, sometimes radically.

In marriage, or any live-in relationship, you range back and forth all the time between your alone self and your social self.

The impact of this flux can be dramatic. In Ned's case, for example, its impact was extreme:

Before I married Sue, I had written no books, fathered no children, created no financial stability, had no spiritual practice, and teetered on and off the edge of sadness most days. My alone self didn't lead me in productive directions. Sure, I had completed college and medical school, done a residency and fellowship, and started a private practice, but I was not fulfilled. Not by a long shot.

Even though it was a sad self, my alone self lured me in because it was a safe place to be. It put no demands on me. I wanted to go there when I had free time. Alone, I could feel whatever I wanted to feel. I didn't have to put on a happy face. I didn't have to say anything smart. Alone, I didn't have to please anyone else. Alone, I could watch TV and not need to be clever or productive. Alone, I could do whatever I wanted, even if it wasn't much.

But then, at the age of thirty-nine, I married Sue. For two events in my life, I totally miscalculated their impact. Going in, I had no idea what a profound effect either of these would have upon me. The first was marrying Sue. The second was having children. They are the two most fulfilling, life-transforming steps I've ever taken.

After I married Sue, twenty years ago, my life completely changed. But the change was not directed by me. It just happened, not according to any plan I'd made. That's why I think of my marrying Sue as an unexpected gift, just as having children would soon also be. I think in most marriages such an unexpected gift gets given and received.

When I married Sue, I remember a close relative looking at me toward the end of the wedding reception and commenting, "You look confused." She was right. I was confused. I hoped all would turn out for the best, but I surely wasn't certain. Just the day before the wedding I had bought a pair of shoes for the ceremony. When I told the woman selling me the shoes they were for my wedding, she said, "My condolences. I hope yours turns out better than mine did."

Of course, I got married with high hopes. I did not feel anything like the woman in the shoe store—although that woman haunts most weddings. But I truly did not know what the years ahead would hold for Sue and me. I was, as the guest had observed, confused.

Then, guided by forces beyond my control, the unexpected gift began to unwrap itself, spontaneously and unplanned. I was not in charge, directing each step. As far as I knew, I was just going about my usual life, only now with Sue.

But my usual life vanished. I began to write books and we began to have children—we now have three. We got pets. I began to build some financial security, and I found the courage to strike out on my own professionally in ways I hadn't dared do before. I left the security of academics, realizing it was stultifying for me. I reached out to public audiences, knowing those were the people I wanted to touch.

Sue and I started attending church together, the same church that we attend to this day. All of our kids were baptized there. It has become a spiritual home for us.

As I look back, I often wonder what it was about getting married and having children that was so extraordinarily life-changing. I had been married before, to a wonderful woman, but that marriage was not meant to last. We were married for a year and parted amicably. So it is not simply "being married" that works the kind of transformation that overcame me.

Nor was the transforming effect of marriage upon me due to lightning-bolt romantic love. I didn't feel as if I had found the "perfect" woman at whose feet I could worship every day. In fact, Sue was the last person I thought I'd marry. She was from the South, she was stable and kind, she was happy. I was none of those. I always thought I would marry a neurotic New Englander, some tortured writer-in-the-making, or some beautiful socialite whose Brahmin family would take the place of the family I lost growing up. We all have these imagined life scripts. In my mind, I would marry a poetic, blue-blooded, passionate soul. I didn't know exactly what that meant, but I envisioned a character out of F. Scott Fitzgerald's short stories or *The Great Gatsby*.

I was a naïve, foolish romantic, headed straight for the kind of destruction that befell most of the characters Scott Fitzgerald created, not to mention Fitzgerald himself. I was dating various women— wonderful women, none exactly out of the Fitzgerald mold, therefore none that I was ready to marry—and having a grand old time, but I had no idea where I was headed.

Then the strangest thing happened, almost as if without my conscious participation in it. It all started when something caught my attention (remember . . . love begins in attention). One day I saw a straw hat with a red hatband sitting on the shelf above the backseat beneath the rear window of a car parked in the lot of the hospital where I worked. I saw that red hatband and I said to myself, "I want to go out with whoever owns that hat." I had no memories of red hatbands, they symbolized nothing special to me, but that red hatband all but reached up out of the car and grabbed me.

Because the cars in that lot had to have parking stickers, I was able to look up who owned the car, which was a young social worker named Sue George.

I asked her out. She said no. I asked her out again. She said yes.

Soon after, we went to a party at a school where I was consulting. An elderly lady who taught at the school was at the party, but I don't recall speaking to her that evening. However, when I was at the school the next day, she came up to me and asked, "When are you going to marry that wonderful woman you were with last night?"

Something clicked. When I left the school, I drove straight to a jewelry store that has special meaning to me because my mother once dated one of its founders. I thought of her when I entered the store that day, and I smiled knowing how much she would have liked Sue. I bought an engagement ring, planned a trip to Paris, and days later proposed at a restaurant in Neuilly I couldn't afford. Sue said yes.

It wasn't a bolt of romantic love that led me to do it. It wasn't from the Fitzgerald script at all. The force of true connection, not the deception of romance, led me to make the best decision I've ever made. It was as if I obeyed gravity. As to what led Sue to say yes, whenever I've asked her that question, she simply replies, "I loved you."

Upon reflection now, I can say it wasn't just chance that brought us together. At the time it seemed like chance. But as I reconstruct it, I can remember all along having respected Sue George. We had worked at the same hospital for several years before we went out. She wasn't the type I had in mind, so I hadn't asked her out, but I believe the still, small voice that speaks to all of us deep inside was waiting for the right time to speak up and get me to do what it knew would be best. My part was to listen to the voice inside me saying, "Ask her out again," when Sue first refused me. Listen to the voice and act in a way some would call impulsive.

———

Once we were married, we started having children right away, which only fueled the force of connection in the house we bought. When our first child, Lucy, was born, I entered permanent psychosis. I fell crazy in love with this little baby. Just as I fell in love with our next child, Jack, and then Tucker.

Starting with the marriage, leading to our having three children over the next six years, we created a force field of connection the like of which I had never lived within during my previous thirty-nine years of life.

This force field—not anything Sue or I did on our own—worked the dramatic change I underwent after we got married.

My alone self didn't disappear or even change all that much. When I'm alone in hotel rooms, I still fight to stave off sadness. But now, instead of just ordering room service or watching TV, I can sometimes write or maybe go work out or even visit a museum. Old sorrow still stalks me, but it no longer holds me back, nor does it define me as it used to. This small sad part of who I am is not altogether bad, in that it allows me to understand more viscerally the sadnesses of other people.

Under the influence of the force field of connection, I became far more productive than I'd ever been and far happier.

I tell my story here because I believe *any* marriage can generate such a force field. In no way do I regard my example as exceptional or unavailable to other people. Just the opposite. I believe it is available to everyone. That's the great good news. Everyone can create such a transformative force field of love and connection. You don't have to be married to do it; any couple can create this positive force field.

And you can still argue, disagree, get mad, pout, slam doors, feel rejected, want to reject, feel lost, feel empty, not know which end is up, worry, fret, feel as if you're with the wrong person, take antidepressants, entertain fantasies about other men or women, feel envious of others, bear grudges, in short, do all the things that make us human.

The force field of connection does not depend upon perfection or anything close to it. The white picket fence, the greenest of green lawns, the ideal children, the golden retriever, and the minivan are props in a cliché of a movie.

Real marriage—real closeness—real connection—is messy. It is imperfect. It starts in the foul rag-and-bone shop of the heart.

When people get close, they look to each other to make things better, and they blame each other when things go wrong. When people get close, they often hurt each other. The goal is simply to help more than hurt.

The positive force of connection grows as long as the people involved pump their best energies into it. As long as they *try* to care for the other person, their mistakes and failures won't ruin the field. The connection will deepen and grow.

More than anything else, tapping into all that connection can do to help you lead a better life depends upon your trusting in the power of love. As the old saying goes, whether you believe it's true or not, love takes work. But no work pays off better, or in more surprising ways. Investing your most loving energy in the person you're with and your children, if you have them, and investing loving energy in your friends and in all other connections that matter deeply to you—this is the recipe for the most joyful and useful life.

———

Loving energy drives me to write books—and drives most people to do whatever they do if they love to do it. It is ironic that I write to connect with others but, like most writers, do all my writing alone. I usually have music playing, but while I write, I am in the company of no other person except myself. Yet my books have provided me with some of my richest and most sustaining connections . . . with people I have never and will never meet.

I think what I do as a writer serves as a kind of model for what a marriage or any close relationship takes in.

I begin alone, with a blank page. Then I start to feel something and think something. Words follow.

A relationship begins with a person being alone. Then he starts to feel something and think something and actions follow. He reaches out. He connects.

As the relationship grows, we get wrapped up in activities, shared memories, shared friends, favorite foods and movies, preferred temperatures, and all the details that comprise the daily stuff of two people together. With today's world of overload, that *stuff* is ever more copious.

But I wonder, is there not an element in every intimate relationship of the writer sitting alone in his study, imagining the audience he is connecting with? Is there not also an element in every relationship of the writer sitting alone in his study feeling comfortable, or uncomfortable, with who he is within himself?

It is a commonplace that most writers are conflicted, if not tortured, individuals. It may be argued that if a writer didn't feel uncomfortable within himself, he would never write, because writing is so difficult and unforgiving a task.

I think it could also be argued that if each of us didn't feel uncomfortable within ourselves, we would never marry, because marriage is so difficult and unforgiving a task!

It is often said that you can't love another person until you love yourself. I disagree. I know quite a few people who love themselves so much that they *can't* love another person.

Just as, on some level, pain (which is a part of loving energy) drives me to write, on some level pain drives us all to connect. Both writing and connecting can be so frustrating and difficult that one must be exceptionally motivated to undertake either.

I'm talking about something long. Anyone can write a short sentence or have a brief conversation. What's difficult is the writing of a book, or the sustaining of an intimate relationship over time.

At the heart of what makes writing so difficult is the inexactitude of getting what is in your head onto a page. At the heart of what makes a relationship so difficult is the inexactitude of explaining who you are and what you need.

Then, of course, there is the pesky little question of who will care enough to listen. When I write, I have to worry, will anyone care enough to read these words?

In love, we have to worry, will he/she care enough to try to understand who I am and meet my needs? Will I care enough to do the same in return?

This bridging of the gap from aloneness to duality depends upon each person feeling enough pain, joy, fear, hope, commitment, and everything else that people feel in love, to work the work, to do what it takes . . . to write the words, to edit the page, to take the chance that no one will listen, and still send out the messages anyway.

If we each do that, if we each commit to the effort, then, I believe, we activate an as-yet-unnamed force that animates life (and perhaps defies death).

Abundant evidence exists of such a force in life. For example, social isolation is as dangerous a risk factor for early death as smoking cigarettes. People who maintain friendships and attend meetings of clubs and other groups not only live longer than those who do not but report much higher feelings of well-being as well as better health statistics. In identifying which children will not get into trouble as they grow up, defining trouble as violent behavior, academic failure, drug or alcohol abuse, unwanted pregnancy, or suicidal thoughts or gestures, the most salient predictors are their feelings of a positive connection at home and at school. In studies of immune function, it has been shown that people who maintain strong attachments to others get sick less easily and, when they do get sick, get better faster than those who live more isolated lives.

That's just a taste of the abundant evidence of the power of the force field of connection.

A loving relationship with another person is by no means the only way to create and tap into this force field, but it is one reliable and potent way to do it. It is one way to unwrap the unexpected gift this all-powerful force field can bestow.

TWENTY-ONE

Finding Hope

Five of the worst words a person can hear are "I don't love you any-more." They sound like a great door closing. Hearing those words can feel like an ambush or a surprise attack. It feels unfair, but is so subjective that it can't be argued with. It rings with such deflating fi-nality that the sentence invites no natural reply. What can you say? "Gee, that's too bad" or "Why?"

We'd like to help you never to hear those words, or if you have heard them or uttered them, find hope. Because there is hope. There is always hope, realistic, can-happen hope. As long as you are alive, there is hope. The real question is, how to find it? It is there, I know that for sure, but *it is often hidden.*

We've worked with many couples who, when they first come to see one of us, have told us they have lost all hope. They were consulting one of us as a last resort, but they held little or no hope that their re-lationship would endure. As we've listened to them argue with each other in our offices, we've found ourselves wondering if maybe they were correct. Maybe their situation was hopeless. Maybe they would be better off apart. After all, not all couples should stay together.

But then, each of us has reminded our respective selves that they wouldn't have come to see us if they didn't harbor some hope for a better future. Maybe that future would include divorce, but they had to have some slim hope for a better future simply because they were sitting in our office trying to get to a better place. It was not our job to determine whether they should divorce but rather to help them both in their search for hope, for a happier life. Our job was to engage with them in a process that goes under the deceptively simple name *therapy*.

We've learned to trust the *process*, not aim toward a specific outcome, be it staying together, getting divorced, trying a period of separation, or whatever outcome one might envision. We provide a place to meet, a start time and an end time, safety, certain questions and suggestions, a predictable structure, and other bits and pieces. The process is what matters. It's larger than the people involved. If you follow the right process, the little boat we create turns into a great ship that brings you to a safe shore. Whatever shore you reach will feel like the right one.

Just as in therapy, a process evolves in a marriage (or other relationship). However, we don't talk about or define the process of a marriage the way we talk about and define, say, the process of therapy.

We ought to. Many couples today don't give themselves a chance to endure as a couple because they don't create and follow a sensible process. They don't abide by the basic rules of sound couples' hygiene, so to speak. They don't spend time together, they don't pay attention to one another, they don't exchange gifts or soft glances, they take each other's love for granted, they make insufficient effort to resolve differences, they get sidetracked by careers, and then, one day, one of them drops a bombshell and says, "I don't love you anymore," or, more commonly, one day one of them quietly notices that no joy or passion is left in the relationship.

At that point they explain what's happened with sad, generic concepts such as "falling out of love," "growing past each other," "not needing each other now that the kids are gone," or "losing the magic," while, in fact, neither member of the couple has any idea *specific* to their relationship of what went wrong.

Usually, the process went wrong. A series of countless little things, not one or two big things, went wrong. And if one or two big things did go wrong, those one or two big things were usually the result of a series of many little things. *The little things are what make up the process.*

We know the word *process* sounds dry as dust, but the meaning of it teems with energy and practical applications once you understand how we're using it. The point of having a process is to prevent the series of little things from going wrong. Just as an airline pilot runs down a checklist before he or she takes off to prevent some little thing from making a big thing go wrong, so a marriage needs a process that prevents all the little things from going wrong that bring about the big thing. These days, it's harder than ever to stick to such a process because the forces of distraction are so potent.

To understand what we mean by a process, just think of where you work. Most people have a process at work (or at school). When they arrive at the door, or even before they get there, they enter the process. It includes a setting where they do their work, a routine, a schedule, clear lines of communication, a job description, designated assistants and reports, well-defined steps for dealing with conflicts and unexpected developments, and all the rest that makes up the complex process of a workplace.

Couples cobble together some kind of makeshift process, but they usually just patch it together piecemeal. They don't have a strategy (while businesses invest millions developing a strategy). They don't decide upon their process, they just let it evolve. Who does the dishes, who pays the bills, who kisses whom good-night first, who takes the kids to the doctor, who says a blessing before a meal or who decides that a blessing will not be said, who plans vacations, who offers compliments, who complains first about the temperature, who decides how the money gets spent and saved—the list is lengthy indeed. But rarely is the process at home anywhere nearly as well-defined as it is at work.

Which is fine, up to a point. You certainly don't want a manual of policies and procedures for your marriage. A strategic planning meeting for marriage would be rather stilted (albeit perhaps productive). But, if you are married to distraction, paying attention to the process of your marriage could help you more than you might imagine.

Usually trouble begins in the breach of the little things, the breach of proper process. One person does one set of dishes too many. One birthday too many gets forgotten. One sneeze too many gets ignored. One hairdo too many goes unnoticed, one romantic overture too many gets rebuffed, one late night at work too many gets spent—all these kinds of little things combine to create A Big Problem.

Paying no attention to the process can lead to tragic results. More commonly, inattention to the process leads to the repetitive disappointments and miscommunications that strew the grounds of most unhappy marriages.

The solution is to take charge and create the process yourselves, not let it spring up around you like weeds. It isn't just division of labor that defines the process, although that matters a great deal. It is also about your hopes and expectations. It is about how you both handle the following issues (and many more):

- offering and asking for compliments
- noticing the other person's appearance
- cuddling
- housework
- shopping
- style of raising children
- sleep
- exercise
- making sure the other person feels valued and respected
- what you do when you feel undervalued or disrespected
- flowers
- food
- celebrations
- God
- what happens right after you arrive at home after work
- getting out the door in the morning

- the use of swears and four-letter words
- timeliness
- getting lost in the car
- one person's desire for certain sexual practices the other person doesn't love to give or receive
- the use of leisure time
- how you deal with unexpected good or bad news

This list is just a start. We offer it just to prime your imaginative pump, as a guide for a discussion you might have. It is useful for couples to discuss the process they've developed, then to modify it as much as is needed for each to get his or her needs and desires met every day, if that's possible. For example, instead of reacting with anger when you feel neglected, you might have the following discussion proactively:

WIFE: I know giving compliments doesn't come naturally to you, but I need compliments.

HUSBAND: I know. Don't I give you enough of them?

W: Well, no, you actually do not. I understand this is hard for you, and I do not want to put you on the defensive, but I don't want to be asking for compliments when I need them. If you could just make a point of complimenting me more often, I think you'd find me happier, and when I'm happier, we both know you're happier.

H: So, like, I should tell you you look pretty and your dress looks great and your figure is outstanding?

W: Yes! Exactly. Especially about the figure.

H: And how often should I do this?

W: More often than you do now.

H: But I already think I do it a lot.

W: Yes, I know. So you need to lay it on, what you would consider *thick*. You need to do it, what might seem to you a ridiculous amount. You don't need to do it as often as you check your email, but it would be nice for me to feel you notice me, say, one-hundredth as much as you notice your email.

H: I get the idea.

W: Thanks for not being defensive. Now, what would you like me to do more often for you?

H: Well, I think we both know one answer to that question.

W: Mmmm. Okay. And what else?

H: Well, honestly, I'd like it if you didn't make me feel guilty every time I go play golf.

W: Good point. You're right. I get resentful. The best way to prevent that is for us to agree in advance how much golf is going to get played. Make it so we agree in advance. Can we do that?

H: But how about when I just want to grab my clubs and take the boys and spontaneously go play?

W: That's fine, as long as you don't do it too much.

H: How much is too much?

W: You'll know by my reaction.

This is an example of process being discussed and negotiated. It may seem simple, but we have learned over years of working with people, the simplest interventions work the best.

———

In addition to a process, which in its details is mundane, you also need a dream. Your dream is not mundane. Your dream sets your direction. You follow your dream. The dream supplies the magic, the romance, the energy, that drives the process.

For example, the dream that drives our marriage is to give our children the happy childhood we didn't have.

What drew us to each other from the beginning was our shared dream of creating a childhood as ideal as we could for the kids we hoped to have. We have pursued that dream tenaciously. That dream has guided all our major decisions, from where we live to how we spend our money to what we do for vacations to our religious practice, to what we eat and how we decorate our house. Ned makes far less money than he might in order to be there for the kids. Sue stayed home and gave up what would have been a stellar career in order to be the best mom she could. She works part-time and has had an excellent career as a therapist, but she is not the famous person she would have been had she gone full bore into a career. We don't regret any of these decisions because they were all guided by our dream.

If you combine attention to the process of your marriage with an abiding pursuit of the dream you share, you will never fall out of love. And you will always find hope, even when you're down. You will have your good days and bad days, you will fight from time to time, you will have moments of being angry at, disliking, or even hating your spouse for a moment or a day, but you will always find your way back into the process and the dream.

Your marriage will grow and deepen, contained by the process, fueled by the dream. The dream may enlarge and change, the process may alter in its details, but the marriage will grow in its life-giving powers.

You will wake up one random morning and see your mate lying sound asleep next to you, and you will smile. This smile is one of the most triumphant and jubilant smiles you can ever smile, even though no one sees it. Smiling that quiet smile as you gaze at your sleeping partner, you feel that you've done a very good thing being with this person, you've become one lucky human, you've found a fine way in this often not-so-fine and treacherous world, you've been blessed with a bond you had no right to expect nor have you done much to deserve. But by keeping at it, by letting yourself stay together long enough to know you're not going anywhere else, even though there could have been elsewheres to go, by siding with connection rather than distraction, by doing what you had to do to make this connection work, and, better than that, by allowing it to take you places you hadn't been before, places of trust in the midst of anger and love in the midst of sadness, by going to bed and waking up together day after day, by becoming more and more mindful of who that other person is and what a joy and pain in the butt he/she has turned into for you; you find one of the rarest feelings to be had in modern life, a feeling of stability in the midst of chaos, and you wake up in the presence of one of the purest pleasures and most fortifying forces anyone ever feels in this life. You wake up to lasting love.

TWENTY-TWO

What Makes It Worthwhile

Love is easy to understand when it's love at first sight. It's when two people have been looking at each other for years that it becomes a miracle.

—SAM LEVENSON

Throughout this book, we have extolled the value of connection. We have touted positive connection and the force field it creates as the single most powerful tool we have to create a healthy life, a long life, a happy life, a productive life, and a moral life. We have recommended "connectedness" as the magic bullet, the key to all that is best in this world, and we have dubbed disconnection the single most common cause of misery, underachievement, anxiety, depression, substance abuse, immoral behavior, ill health, and even suicide.

But, for the sake of truth in advertising, we must admit that we also know that connecting intimately with another person can be, well, like connecting intimately with a nest of angry hornets. No matter how good a person you are, no matter how good the person you're with may be, intimacy activates parts of us we usually suppress in the name of politeness and social graces. When you marry, you give up your usual hiding places, while the person you're with tries to ferret you out of them.

When you marry, you often start to blame the other person for everything that's wrong with your life, you start to look to the other person to supply everything that's missing, and you cease to extend to the person you married all the sweets and endearments you bestowed before that fatal day in church, under the chuppah, or wherever you took your vows.

So what in the world makes it worthwhile?

I, Ned, once heard a sermon about the people "who walk by with no intention of ever coming into this church, or any church. Indeed, they are resolutely opposed to the very existence of church, and they walk past us as if we were a danger to society."

What the minister said was surprising. He said, "I envy those people." He envied them because they do not have to suffer the pain the possibility of God inflicts. Once you walk into a church or its equivalent, once you open yourself up to the possibility of God, once you decide to search further than the answer atheism provides, then you step into a holy mess. You get confused. You feel awestruck, but in a way that does not necessarily feel good. It's akin to the awe you feel when you look up into the night sky and try to imagine infinity. It makes you ache with incomprehension.

When you walk into the world of the spirit, you get filled with hope and doubt, you feel called but unworthy, you feel giddy but afraid, ecstatic but wary of the letdown, you feel as if you were rooted in quicksand, as if faith were a near impossibility you are trying to develop with all your heart and all your soul and all your mind.

When you walk in, when you commit to taking God seriously, if not actually believing, you also join legions of people you want no part of. You join legions of hypocrites, zealots, and prigs. You meet people you don't like. You are assumed to believe without question things you most certainly do question. It is all quite upsetting and confusing. It makes you wonder why you ever wandered in.

A lot like getting married. A lot like walking into the world of love.

When you walk into *that* place, when you take *those* vows, when you give up the freedom of the people who quickly walk on by, you walk into a similar mess with similar feelings.

You feel confused and awestruck, filled with hope and doubt, you feel called but unworthy, giddy but afraid, ecstatic but wary of the let-down, you feel rooted in quicksand, as if marriage were a state you are trying to believe in with all your heart and all your soul and all your mind.

When you marry, you also join legions of hypocrites, zealots, prigs, and other people you don't like. You are assumed to believe without question things you most certainly do question. It is all upsetting and confusing.

So why do either? Why walk in?

There are many reasons, but the most compelling reason is the hope that two is so much better than one that it's worth whatever downside there might be. In the case of love, two people. In the case of faith, you plus whatever you put your faith in.

Imagine the possibility. If there truly is a God, well, you can fill in that blank for yourself. It is likely the most significant "if" statement any of us ever encounters.

The hope, the possibility inherent in marriage, or any love relationship, is a close second. What makes prolonged intimacy so compelling, so worth trying, is the possibility it offers. If you can truly create a good marriage, well, you can fill in that blank, too. What *you* hope for in marriage may be quite different from what either of us hopes for. We each have different wounds to heal, different pasts to reconcile, different alone selves we live with, different satisfactions to seek. But it's safe to say that we all hope for happiness and a better life than we would have were we not married.

When your experience with faith or with marriage doesn't work out, those two disappointments are parallel as well. When faith fails you, or when marriage fails you, each usually does so for similar reasons.

Faith collapses or a marriage collapses, usually, because of pain. Great pain can overwhelm hope. It can overwhelm faith or a human connection. The pain in the incongruity between what is offered (by faith, by marriage) and what is delivered (by faith, by marriage) grows too severe to bear. It hurts too much to hope any longer. A person leaves his faith or leaves his marriage in a last-ditch effort to end, or at least reduce, the pain that continued faith or marriage appears inevitably to entail.

It is a paradox that both faith and marriage purport to make life more bearable, but they both end because of how unbearable the pain of life can be.

Sometimes it works. Sometimes giving up hope and leaving your faith or leaving your marriage makes you happier. Sometimes it doesn't. In either case, people continue to search for what they need, only elsewhere. Sometimes they find it, sometimes they don't, but the need for love continues.

Loving a real-life, flesh-and-blood human being may seem totally different from loving an unseen, untouchable spirit, but to do one is to do the other. You can't see your partner's soul or spirit, yet you love it as much as, if not more than, his or her visible parts. The heart of both faith and marriage is love. Love yokes the two.

Once you open yourself up to love, you open yourself up not only to a passionate, messy connection with a living person, you also open up that part of yourself that lets God in, even if you do not call the force that fills you God. You do not need to have a formal spiritual belief to be connected to God. All you have to do is love.

Such feeling sidesteps doubt and debate. When you love, you *know* that you love. You may fear losing the person you love, you may suffer pain, you may fear that person doesn't love you back, you may fear that you don't deserve the love or that it will not last, but you do not doubt the feeling itself, any more than you doubt what you feel from a fire as you sit in front of it.

When you think of your spouse or your child or many of your friends, you may fear for them, but you shouldn't doubt what you feel for them. It is that feeling that gives life meaning and makes it worthwhile.

Cynicism is the result of giving up hope and shutting down. Pain shuts off hope. Cynicism is disappointed hope. But if you can summon the courage to remain open and vulnerable, you will find a connection that will lead you to a renewal of hope and, in turn, love. Perhaps it will not be love for and from the person you want, but it will be love.

The supply of love in life is infinite. As long as you keep yourself open to it, you'll find it or it will find you.

Love may not walk up to you and announce in a trumpet voice, "Here I am, come to save you." But if you incline your imagination toward what cannot be seen or heard, you will find it.

A poet wrote, "Heard melodies are sweet but those unheard are sweeter." When we reach out into the world that lies beyond knowledge and proof, we find the greatest prizes.

But what if you hear nothing? What are you to do if try as you might, you feel no hope? What are you to do if you feel unloved and out of love to give? What are you to do if advice like "summon the courage to remain open" sounds like empty words?

At that moment, believe it or not, love is close to you. Paradoxical, indeed preposterous, as it may sound, when you are in the depths, love is close by. When you have put aside all the diversions and trinkets we use to avoid the worst in life, then you are most ready to open up to the best. Now is the time to be patient. *Patient* literally means "the power of suffering." Now is the time to refrain from taking destructive action, the worst, of course, being taking your own life.

If you can wait, the suffering will pass. The reason we hospitalize suicidal patients against their will is not because we want to impose our will upon theirs, but because we have learned many times over that, with a few exceptions, the desire to die disappears if you keep a person alive.

But if you are in despair and you are reading these words, your response will likely be "Shut up, you windbags! You have no clue as to how I feel or how hopeless my situation is. I've lost everything, and you're telling me to put up with it. You call that help?"

And we would say, "Let's keep talking." As long as you're angry, we're connected. The sign of disconnection is not anger, it is indifference. Even if you feel indifferent, even if you have lost all hope and truly do not care what happens next, help is on the way. You don't have to believe it, you just have to stay alive long enough for it to reach you. If you can reach out, even better. But if you can't, just hold on. Your life will take a turn for the better.

How do we know this? Because we have seen it many times over.

We have seen people in the absolute depths of despair, people who were convinced that not only was their own life worthless but that life itself was worse than worthless, it was a cruel and painful joke. And we have seen these people weeks and months later giving thanks that they didn't take drastic action when they felt their worst.

We can't claim to know how it happens, but we do know that it happens because we have seen it many times. Hope and love will reach you, one way or another, if you let them. Even as you try to fight them off, say by attacking the person who shows up to help, you begin to let them in. You don't have to believe in love—or anything else—for it to help you. All you have to do is stay alive long enough for it to reach you.

Most of you reading this book are nowhere near despair, but the same principles apply. If you feel out of love in your marriage, or so distracted that you can't give or receive as much love as you'd like, don't shut down. Get angry. Go off half-cocked. Just stay in the hunt. Keep searching. Your search will be answered. Likely not in the way you hope or expect, but in a good way nonetheless. Love surprises us all.

How many people leave a relationship or a marriage before they find the next good surprise? They give reasons like:

"He's just not Mr. Right."

"What can I say, she doesn't do it for me any longer."

"We're miserable together. It's time to make a change."

"He's so into himself, he can't be into me."

"She's a great person, but she doesn't turn me on like she used to."

"He's hurt me too much. There's no making it good again."

"I'm still waiting, but the right guy just hasn't come along."

"When I look at her now, I feel nothing."

"He's not the man I married. The love is gone."

"Happy marriage is a fairy tale."

Just as in the extreme example of a suicidal patient, the key for the person who wants to leave either a relationship or a belief is to wait. Of course, at times it is dangerous to wait. If you are in danger, leave. But otherwise, wait a bit. Keep the search alive. If you do leave, don't cease your search.

The keys to each—a relationship or faith—are patience and persistence. The spiritual connection develops as you reach out further than you can see and try to connect to what lies beyond knowledge. The loving connection develops as you see more in the other person than he or she sees in him- or herself. Both involve your seeing more than is visible. *This is hard to do rationally.* How do you connect to what is beyond knowledge or out of sight? What's there to connect to? How do you connect to nothing? You use your imagination. You welcome what lies beyond reason. Both love and faith depend upon imagination. It's not like going to the movies and waiting for the movie to move you. *You* move you. *You give in*—to love or to faith—even though both seem a bit crazy. Then the unheard melody starts to play.

We are not talking about acting out of obligation. Neither the spiritual connection nor the marital connection can be helped by reciting a list of promises or beliefs. The spiritual connection is not about dogma or creed. It is not about memorizing the Ten Commandments. Indeed, that can be counterspiritual. As a prayer puts it, "Lord, help me always to search for the truth, but spare me the company of those who have found it."

The spiritual connection is, by definition, the connection to what is *not* known and what *can't* be proven. It is necessarily enshrouded in uncertainty and mystery.

The same applies to love here on earth. While we know the person we marry, while we see him or her, while we touch and caress, smell, hold, and hear that person, that person remains, at some level, forever separate, forever mysterious.

Developing the possibility inherent in any marriage is like developing the possibility inherent in the spiritual connection. It depends upon seeking, upon reaching, upon finding nothing or even finding what you don't want to find, and still coming back to look again. How foolish, huh? You have to be a bit of a fool either to fall in love or to find God. As Shakespeare wrote, the lunatic, the lover, and the poet are all of a piece.

Both love and faith require lunacy perhaps, but persistence for sure, especially persistence in the face of disappointment. That's when the human spirit earns its stripes, when it refuses to give up even though all is long since lost. When all that's left is to carry on, to carry on then with hope and humor is to poke a hole in the joke of life. No one should die without having done that. That's when you find out the joke is no joke. It's a far better deal than you thought.

Both love and faith depend upon accepting the resounding emptiness and aloneness we all can feel when we look up into the night sky, and yet, still, even so, in spite of it all, no matter what . . . finding some connection, however phantasmagoric, between your aloneness and some other person, or the spiritual world.

———

Marriage may join us hand in hand, but we still must take our solitary ways. Neither marriage nor any spirit can change that we each live, to some extent, alone.

But to what extent? That's the pesky question hope poses. It is to what extent that makes both the possibility of marriage and the possibility of a spiritual connection so compelling—sometimes ecstatic.

Developing both takes work. They take a reaching out, a willingness to get hurt, feel inadequate, be disappointed over and over. Both require persistent hope in the face of disappointment. Both require that you not take your life at face value. Both require that you try to see what you can't see, to see what is blurred, what is not visible, what many people (including you sometimes) would say doesn't even exist, what cannot be divined by any scientific instrument that we have: the essence of another person, or the presence of God.

The rustic instruments we *can* use reside in what the poet William Butler Yeats called "the foul rag-and-bone shop of the heart." In our age, we reject or trivialize the power of these instruments. If we can't measure or test or prove an idea, then it is not worthy of our attention. We live in an age that demands proof based upon empirical evidence. The rest is hogwash.

How desperately we need that hogwash!

———

Let's say you agree. Let's say you want more than what the measured data can prove. Let's say you are willing to use the instruments in the rag-and-bone shop. Let's say you're a good sport and you're willing. You're ready. Your only question is, how? Where do I find *those* instruments? How do I use them? And how in the world can I trust them?

They are the instruments we've been talking about throughout this book: attention, focus, empathy (which depends upon imagination), curiosity and an inquiring attitude, the ability to listen, patience, and a willingness to enter into, if not trust, a process more powerful than you and your brain.

These instruments are at hand. *They reside within you now, and always have.* You developed them growing up, and you've never lost them. They may be rusty due to lack of use, but you could sit down with your spouse right now and say, "Tell me about your day," only *this* time do it with true focus, rapt attention, a genuinely inquiring heart, ears that are primed to hear what isn't said, and an imagination eager to extend itself into the reality your spouse will present.

"Aw, c'mon," you say. "Get real. Like I'm gonna do *that?*" Or she/he's gonna do that?

You could. He could. She could. At any given moment, until there are no more moments to give, we all could. The possibility is at hand every second. Right up until the end, we could.

This is the possibility in any intimate relationship. We *can* probe past the boundaries of our aloneness. We can try to find what we seek even knowing we will never see it revealed as clearly as the sun or the moon or the stars.

Of course, if we do it, if we reach out in naked, stupid vulnerability, we risk the connection going wrong, sometimes horribly wrong. When you reach out, there's no guarantee what you'll find. It's not like fairy tales. The other person may be tired, in a bad mood, not in the frame of mind to reach back, or just not much interested in you right then. You can encounter what we call "empathic failures," which is shrink-speak for devastatingly disappointing moments of the other person not responding in the way you need him or her to.

For example, one of us might say to the other, "I had this amazing, incredible experience today that really changed my life," and the other might reply, "It is so hot in this house, I just can't stand it." The person who had the great day feels rebuffed, put down, and demeaned. He—since in this case it was Ned—feels as if his treasure has just been spat upon. In a second, he'll career back through every bitter disappointment in his life. Sue's reaction made him feel totally alone, as if all the years of marriage have just been decimated and he is a man left unto himself. He is in despair.

How could Sue have been so unaware, so uncaring, so uninterested? Simple. She was having a hot flash. Her personal reality was too intense for her to ignore. All she could focus on was how hot she felt. She didn't even hear Ned's words.

I, Ned, can respond by flying into a rage or falling into a pout. I can write pages in my mind about how our marriage is a farce and plan a divorce. I can berate Sue for how selfish she is, or I can feel sorry for myself being in such a loveless marriage.

Or, I can do none of those. *I can trust in the process we have created.* I can trust that as disappointed as she made me feel, it will pass, and that she probably had a good reason for being so uncaring. I can remember who she is, and I can reach out to that person. I can remember the dream we share and take hope from that.

We bring the issue into the petty details of everyday life in an everyday marriage—our own marriage—because that's where these lofty issues play out every day— in the foul rag-and-bone shop of the heart.

Where life matters most, life's a mess. Artists clean it up for us and create order—in novels, symphonies, plays, paintings, and dance. But we who live it, we live life before it's been cleaned up and made beautiful. We live in a holy mess.

As Sue says, at least once a week, "What is it about this house and all of you? As soon as I clean up and straighten things out, it's a mess all over again."

She's talking, of course, about the physical mess we keep making in the house. But it's also a metaphorical mess. Every day brings new problems, unexpected issues, and unplanned difficulties. Most are simple, such as a parking ticket or a clogged toilet, but some are major, such as an illness, a lost job, a death.

We might as well face it. Life's a mess. It's a relentless mess-in-the-making. We try to tidy up, we try to build shelters and take control, we work our puny plans and schemes, but the mess always lurks. No one has it figured out. Even the fabulously wealthy and the famous suffer, get sick, and die. Even the people who seem most to have it all together lose it altogether.

So what are we to do? Connect.

The main reason to marry or commit to love, as we see it, is to side with hope over despair. Even though despair might make more sense, given the fate we're all heir to, even though we live in a world that proceeds not from pleasure to pleasure but from hope to hope, isn't it better still to hope? And to love even while knowing that you will one day lose the person you love?

Once you decide to live, it is best to live on the side of love and hope while this world wrings the life out of you. To commit to one person is a way to moor that love and know where it will be the next day, unless a storm blows it away. It is also to have someone you can tackle the messes with. Doing it together can make even the worst messes and meaninglessnesses somehow feel worthwhile. Life will beat us down, but it doesn't have to kill our hope, our dream, our connection, our love. Maybe that's what mature love is all about: taking pleasure in doing together what doing alone wouldn't be worth living for.

The most fundamental reason to stay is to make life for both of you better.

This is the great hope, the real possibility that love holds out to us all: to put enough of an end to our aloneness that we can find a better life in togetherness. While we will never lose our aloneness, nor would it be healthy to do so, at least until we die we can find in togetherness a force that lets us endure pain and find joy, a force that can keep us hopeful even in the face of despair, a force that knows nothing of wealth and fame but knows everything of how to defeat demons and create angels.

As we pointed out at the beginning, creating this force does require tools that can be hard to come by in modern life: attention; time; empathy; connection; play. But the great good news is that you, or anyone, can lay claim to those tools simply by resolving to do so.

Since our aim has to be always practical and offer action steps you can use in your daily life, we want to conclude the book with concrete tips, exercises, suggestions, and bits of time-tested wisdom. To provide you with this as economically as possible, we first provide a bulleted

summary of tips, followed by a workbook. The summary brings together in one place many of the tips that have been offered elsewhere
in this book and introduces some new ones. The workbook gives you a
process that you can follow. It shows you how, day by day, you can reclaim the love you once had or deepen the love you have today.

TWENTY-THREE

Ten Reasons *Not* to Get Divorced;
Ten Reasons *To* Get Divorced; and
Forty Ways to Make Your Marriage Great

If you're anything like us, you can read a book all the way through and remember only a couple of facts or ideas, even though you liked the book and agreed with what it had to say.

To help you collect your thoughts, we bring together here many of the tips and suggestions we offered throughout the book. We have also inserted some from audiences that Ned has polled. When he gives talks, he often asks members of the audience to write down their own ideas and suggestions, and they always produce valuable contributions. The suggestions from people other than the authors of this book are marked below with an asterisk.

The first ten suggestions, offered somewhat tongue in cheek, are all ours.

TEN REASONS *NOT* TO GET DIVORCED

1. Wouldn't you rather subsidize your own children's education than your lawyer's?
2. Do you know how much of a hassle it is to move?
3. Divorce can shorten your life, especially if you are a man.
4. If remarriage represents the triumph of hope over experience, divorce represents the triumph of despair over hope.
5. Imagine a rainy Sunday afternoon and you pick up a photo album from the good days. Do you really want to feel what you're going to feel right then?
6. When you go to a movie and you see those awkward scenes of Dad picking up little Joey for "his weekend," do you really want to be in that scene yourself?
7. Do you really want to go through all the rigmarole of people dancing around trying to sort out loyalties, trying to stay friends with you both, but really not being able to do that? Do you want the weird interactions that come up all the time with people who were supposedly friends with both of you, but suddenly change in how they treat you?
8. The kids. You shouldn't stay in a terrible marriage just for the kids, but the kids can sometimes motivate you to try to recapture the love you once had. The kids would like that—how shall we say it?—very much.
9. Promises. We don't know how much promises mean to you. But you did make some promises.
10. Money. It's not just the lawyers. It's the settlement, the alimony, the child support, the selling of property, and on and on. And this money and property and the possessions are not ordinary money and property and possessions. They are radioactive. Every time you touch them, even think of them, you feel a burn.

TEN REASONS *TO* GET DIVORCED

1. You hate her/him and you can see no possible way for that ever to change. You have felt this way for more than ten min-

utes, ten days, even ten weeks. You've got to have felt this way for a long enough time that you know it isn't going to change. In that case, get divorced. It is bad to live in a force field of hatred.

2. Your spouse is repeatedly abusive to you. Don't stay. Get a therapist who understands abuse because it is unlikely you can do this on your own.

3. You have lost all respect for your spouse. You have tried all that you can to get it back, but you know it is gone forever.

4. You feel utterly indifferent to your spouse. You never think about him/her. You are mere roommates. Not only is there no passion, there is no communication, no shared interest, no desire to try to make things better.

5. Your spouse is so abusing drugs or alcohol that he/she is dangerous. He/she rejects all efforts to help. In complete denial, he/she spends days on end in a stupor.

6. Your spouse severely mistreats your children regularly. If repeated efforts to change this behavior fail, then it is time to take your children and leave.

7. Your spouse changes in such a way that he/she becomes mean daily. All the pep and joy is gone. He/she never has a positive word to say about anything, and criticizes everything you and your children do. He/she refuses to see a therapist or to talk to anyone about his/her problem because he/she believes he/she has no problem. Mired in depression, paranoia, anger, and often alcohol abuse, he/she makes everyone close to him miserable. It is time to leave.

8. Your spouse behaves in ways that violate the basic agreements you made when you got married. For example, he/she may be having affairs. Or may control all the money. Or may insist, out of the blue, that the family join a religion they don't want to join or leave a religion they love. These "irreconcilable differences" can be a solid reason to divorce

9. You don't like the temperature he/she insists on setting the thermostat at. This one is a joke, but I put it in because *many* couples do get divorced for reasons equally trivial or even more trivial. "I hate the way he squeezes the toothpaste out of the

tube." "She is *such* a slow driver." "He *never* lets me watch *my* TV shows." "When he went bald, what can I say? I can't be married to a bald man. And hairpieces only make it worse!" Of course, the trivial reasons usually cover some deeper dissatisfaction or conflict.

10. The love is gone. This is the toughest reason to get divorced. I always ask, "Have you done everything you can to bring it back?" Part of the reason for writing this book was to offer plans to bring it back. Our experience is that lost love can often be rediscovered. But, if it can't, then it is likely better for both parties to say farewell.

FORTY WAYS TO MAKE YOUR MARRIAGE GREAT

The overarching goals for a great marriage

- To see clearly what you want in your main relationship and to feel every day that you are getting closer to that vision.
- To relish and enjoy fully what you already have.
- To feel inspired every day by the power of your dream and the opportunity you have to pursue it.

Ways to get there . . .

1. Set in motion the cycle that drives love. First, pay attention.
2. Spend time together.
3. Develop empathy and understanding by asking questions and listening to answers.
4. Through empathy and understanding, build an ever-stronger connection.
5. On the solid rock foundation of that connection, play. Play is the action of love. Disinhibited, free, let yourselves go together. Find new ways to play. You can do it anywhere!
6. Build boundaries to avoid incessant interruptions.
7. Remember that the key to romance is attention. Nothing is as romantic as having someone give you their undivided, sustained attention.

8. Avoid overload and the F-state it creates. Try to preserve C-state instead.

9. Identify the D (distracter) and the O (organizer) roles in your relationship and plan ways to manage them rather than to fight about them.

10. Avoid the "moral diagnosis," i.e., "you are bad," and replace it with understanding.

11. Don't act as if an inspector were coming to your house to grade you on how neat you are.

12. Avoid making psychiatric diagnoses such as narcissist, passive-aggressive, and obsessive-compulsive. Describe, don't diagnose.

13. Learn how to forgive. Forgiving simply means not carrying anger around for a long time. It does not mean you condone the bad deed.

14. Create a shared dream and draw energy and hope from it.

15. Create a *process* for your marriage, a set of habits, rituals, traditions, and daily practices that keep you in touch with each other, making sure you know what's up with each other and that you are tending to each other's needs every day.

Eliminate toxic worry by using the following five steps

16. Never worry alone.
17. Get the facts.
18. Make a plan.
19. Make time for sex. Embrace each other at least once a day.
20. Divide labor evenly, trying to have each person do what he or she likes to do or dislikes doing least.

Special-ize your relationship using the following steps

21. Know what the other person wants and loves and communicate what you want and love.
22. Provide "something extra."
23. Create special traditions and rituals.

24. Be careful to create protected, uninterrupted time for each other.

25. Invest maximum positive energy in special moments with each other.

26. Learn to control anger. Anger should be like a sneeze, brief, clearing the air, then forgotten.

27. Learn to love to hear your spouse express the deepest (even if somewhat uncomfortable, unseemly, mean, paranoid, or whatever) feelings about his or her experiences in the world and in the extended family. Give loving support and feedback.

28. Never let your spouse see you roll your eyes. Contempt breeds contempt.

29. Use "explicit appreciation." We verbalize our appreciation of one another's qualities many times each day. It's like a wonderful drug—a dose of love and appreciation over and over.

30. Have a date night once a week. Even if it just means taking the dog out for a walk together or spending some time at your local Starbucks.

31. Share a passion for your children. Enjoy them. Have fun together.

32. Relate to each other "off the record" of life. Sometimes to get out of the role we play, particularly in disagreements, it helps to look at ourselves as if from the outside.

33. Make no assumption that your spouse can see, hear, feel, or process what is plainly clear to you.

34. Tell your spouse what you need rather than waiting for him/her to guess.

35. Fight fair. This is the only common trait I have found between long-married friends.

36. Take one-half hour after the kids go to sleep and talk about "stuff," not about work, chores, or conflicts, but about stuff you're interested in. Tell stories, ask questions.

37. Find a passion you both can enjoy.

38. Learn about each other's conative style. Go to Kolbe.com and take the test.

39. Fight the force of distraction in the following ways:

- First, become aware of the problem.
- Identify its sources in your environment and eliminate them as much as possible.
- Rediscover conversation.
- Set boundaries. If you don't, as the Law of Modern Life dictates, your time will be taken from you.
- Learn to say no to good ideas, good people, good projects. One of the greatest parts of modern life is the availability of so much. From information to people to ideas, much more is instantly available to us all than ever before in history. But, as we are learning the hard way, you can have way too much of a good thing. If you don't learn to say no to some great possibilities, your life will be overrun by these great possibilities, and they will become like kudzu, choking out all that is good and valuable.

40. Avoid the big struggle by using the following struggle stoppers:

- Spend time together.
- Pay attention to one another.
- Understand yourself and your partner well enough that you can see what lies beneath the struggle.
- Speak your true feelings.
- Know when you feel deprived and speak that feeling.
- When you feel hurt by the other person, ask yourself, "What do I want this pain to turn into?" Your reflexive response is "I want the other person to hurt as much as I do." That is how many struggles begin. Try to rise above that very human tendency to return pain with pain.
- Practice preventive maintenance. Have special times together every week. Even if it is just for a few minutes, try to make your partner feel special.
- When a fight is about to escalate, ask yourself, "Is this worth it?"

- Remember, your effort to be right might include making the other person be wrong, which is humiliating. In a marriage, being right is far less important than being kind.
- When you're stuck, seeing a good therapist can make a huge difference.

Part 4

THIRTY MINUTES,
THIRTY DAYS

A Workbook for Modern Marriage

Our intent throughout has been to make this book practical and useful. A workbook is a fitting culmination to that effort.

Think of this workbook as a diet in reverse. In a diet, you deny yourself what you crave. Here, you will be asked to give yourself what you've been denying yourself and yet you crave.

It is strange, but many people who are married get into a habit of not allowing themselves the very pleasures they so relished when they first got together. At the top of that list, simply, is time together. This workbook will lead you to once again spend that time together. This workbook will help you get back in sync and reclaim the pleasures you may have let slip away, at least somewhat.

You may resist the idea of a workbook, think it's too cumbersome, gimmicky, or hokey, but please, before you toss it aside, stop for a moment. The workbook is simply a way to provide some ideas, some structure, some positive reinforcement, and some direction toward a goal you yourself want: a better relationship with your spouse or partner.

The workbook will require you to get together each day for thirty minutes. Just follow the workbook, one page a day for thirty days. The days do not have to be sequential. If travel, schedules, or other impediments make it impossible to work the workbook every day, that's fine. After each session, simply schedule a convenient time when you can get together for the next session.

When you and your mate have completed the thirty days, you will automatically be in a better place with each other. This "reverse diet" will instill new, positive habits or allow you to rediscover old ones— and you will have fun. Not many diets can make that claim.

———

Each day gives you an exercise to do together. After each exercise, take notes on what you discuss. Just jot down points you want to remember. You don't have to be a stenographer and write everything down. There will be no test! But it will be useful for you to have some means of recording the points you find valuable, memorable, humorous, or worth following up on, so you can refer back later on.

Reading this book has already started you thinking. You're on your way to a better relationship. But now you need a *process*. As we said earlier, you need a dream and a process. You have the dream of a great relationship. Now the workbook offers you a continuation of the process the book began, a way of working toward that dream systematically day after day.

You will need to get your mate on board with this. If you are the only one who has read the book, you might need to sell the idea of doing the workbook. To do that, just say what's in your heart. Use your own words. Let him or her know this process will be enjoyable, different, and will lead you both to a better, happier place. You can't work the workbook alone. It depends upon the involvement of two people—just like a relationship.

So the prelude to working the workbook is getting the attention and "buy-in" of your spouse or partner. You can't start the workbook until that happens. It may take a bit of time. But don't turn this into a struggle! Persuade. Inform. Listen. Empathize. Use what you've learned in the book to initiate the use of the workbook.

Once you decide to go ahead, a few pointers:

1. You're going to need to set aside a half hour together each day to do this. It doesn't have to be the same time every day, but if it can be, that adds a kind of rhythm. And as I stated before, the days do not have to be sequential.

2. The half hour could be in bed in the morning, at the kitchen table in the evening, or anywhere else, anytime. It must, however, be free of interruptions.

3. Bring this book to the sessions together, and be prepared to take notes on each session together.

4. Each day, read ahead to the next day's exercise, as some of them require a bit of preparation.

Then, jump in, have fun, and enjoy the benefits!

DAY 1

Pick a half hour you can spend with each other today, no interruptions, no electronics, no intrusions of any kind.

At first, this may feel a bit awkward, so we will add some structure to each session. But we hope you will develop an increasing ability, as you go through the 30 sessions, to be fully present with each other. We call such interrupted time "present time," and we intend the pun. By being fully present psychologically, you are bestowing a wonderful gift upon the other person.

The exercise for today, the first day of the 30-day program, is simply for each of you to tell the other what you imagine your day will be like tomorrow. What will you do tomorrow. Give some details. Share with your mate information he or she might not already know as to what a typical day is like for you. Feel free to ask questions or simply ask for elaboration as the other person is talking. Feel free to react spontaneously, show surprise or sympathy, or whatever it is you might feel as you hear the description of their day.

The point of this interaction is to help you acquire some information you might not already have as to what your mate does all day and how he or she feels in doing it.

At the end of the session, and at the end of every subsequent session, plan when your next sesson will be.

DAY 2

When you meet today, discuss what you hope these thirty days will bring to your marriage. Discuss with each other the dream you each have for your marriage.

As you do this, try not to blame each other for your marriage not being perfect. No one has a perfect marriage. Every marriage could improve. Give yourselves credit for taking the time to make this organized and concerted effort to bring improvement to your relationship.

Then, enjoy exchanging your respective visions and dreams of how you'd like things to be. Take some notes so you can refer back to your goals and see if you're getting there. People make more progress when they define a goal and monitor progress.

When you are done, don't forget to plan the place and time for the next session.

DAY 3

Before you meet for your present time, think of an object that has great symbolic meaning to you, something that triggers strong, positive emotions in you. For example, if your dad was a carpenter, the object might be a hammer. Or, the object might be your college diploma, or a photo of your grandmother, or it might be a coin someone gave you years ago that you have saved. It can be anything. But it has to be a *thing,* and a thing you now have. You must bring it with you to your present time.

When you meet for present time today, produce the object you brought with you. Take turns explaining to each other why the object has such deep meaning to you and what that meaning is.

Listen to the other person's narrative closely. Try to put yourself in his or her shoes as you hear what the object means. Try to visualize what he or she is describing. Ask questions as they arise, but try to listen more than inquire.

Write down what object each of you brought.

At the end of the time together, don't forget to plan your next session.

DAY 4

Before you meet for your present time today, think of the five smartest decisions you've made in your life. They can relate to anything, from business, to dating, to school, to friends, to hairdos! Just let yourself reflect on these five smartest decisions. Write them down on a piece of paper. Bring that paper with you for your present time.

When you meet, begin by guessing what's on your partner's list. Don't be surprised if you're way off the mark. It is simply useful for each of you to see from the other's perspective.

At the end of the session, plan your time for tomorrow.

DAY 5

Today's exercise is to compose a prayer for your marriage.

Don't worry! You do not have to believe in God to do this, nor does it mean your marriage (or relationship) is in need of prayer, as if it were dying.

You will simply compose words to be spoken to God or whatever power you believe hovers over, beyond knowledge and what can be proven and disproven.

This is a chance to make a brief prayer you can return to in your thoughts from time to time, a prayer you can modify whenever you want, a prayer that sums up what both of you most value, give thanks for, and hope for together.

You only have half an hour, so get started. Brainstorm, jot down words, then turn them into a prayer. It will be short and to the point. It will be from your heart. It will be a great prayer.

Once you have it, write it down.

Don't forget to pick the time and place for the next meeting.

DAY 6

Today, think back to your childhoods.

Share one of the happiest memories you have and one of the saddest. Let yourself remember as many details of each memory as you can. Start off with the sad memory, each of you telling the other.

Then move on to the happy memory, each of you telling the other.

Try to make each of the memories not be a memory you have already shared with your partner.

Write down a note or two about each memory.

Then plan the next session.

DAY 7

Memories again today.

Look back at your entire relationship, from the moment you first met, until today.

Take a few moments in silence together just to let yourselves take that trip back through time.

Now, recount the images you encountered. Happy, sad, angry, blissful, indifferent. Just share with your partner, back and forth, the images that came to mind as you looked back in time.

Sometimes, what you just "happen to remember" gives a clue to what's up in your unconscious. See if you can gain any insight into your current relationship from these "chance" memories.

Plan your next session.

DAY 8

Today, make wishes.

Each of you makes three wishes for your relationship.

They can be big ("I wish for eternal happiness together"), or they can be small ("I wish you would pick your towels up off the bathroom floor").

Remember, the more specific a wish is, the easier it is for the other person to help you make it come true.

Once you've shared your three wishes, write them down.

Don't forget to plan your next session.

DAY 9

Back to your childhoods again today.

Describe to your partner each of the following:

1. The first girl/boy you had a crush on.
2. The best teacher you ever had (through high school).
3. The place you'd go when you wanted to be alone when you were a child.
4. Your most memorable pet.
5. Your grandparents. If you didn't know your grandparents, describe your favorite relative (other than a parent or sibling).

Plan a time and place for your next session.

DAY 10

Today, tell each other what you like about each other.

Go over all the points, large and small, that you like in your partner. From the mole on her neck to the way his hair parts, tell each other everything that you like.

Write down these points.

This is a list you'll both want to keep!

Then plan the time and place for the next session.

DAY 11

Today, talk about your friends.

More specifically, talk only about what you like in your friends. This may be difficult, as friends can be annoying, but limit yourself to discussing only what you enjoy, admire, or look forward to in each friend.

Don't forget to plan the time and place for the next session.

DAY 12

Today, do something together, some physical activity (other than lovemaking) that you both enjoy.

You might take a walk together. Or you might cook something together. Or work in your garden. Or take a bike ride together, or go swimming.

If it's cold outside or raining, the activity will have to be indoors. Maybe build a fire and hang those pictures you've been meaning to. Or rearrange the living room. Anything.

As you do whatever you choose to do, notice how your interaction is different if you are moving. Movement tends to facilitate conversation.

In addition, physical exercise is good for your brain. It makes communication easier.

Don't forget to schedule your next meeting.

DAY 13

Today, get naked.

Of course, you have to have chosen a place to meet that makes this possible.

Once you are both naked, do whatever you'd like to do. You have a half hour. As always, the only requirement is that you pay full attention to the other person and allow no interruptions.

Before you get dressed, schedule the next session.

DAY 14

Before you meet for this session, pick some piece of art that matters deeply to you. I define art broadly to include literature (prose, poetry, anything written), music, sculpture, painting, dance, film, video, origami, anything that is the product of artistic imagination.

Bring this piece of art with you to the session. If it is a piece of music, bring your iPod or some other means of playing all or a bit of the piece of music. If it is a painting or sculpture, bring a photo of it. If it is literature, bring it with you so you can read some of it aloud.

During the session, share some or all of what you brought, as time allows. You should save time to discuss the other person's selection, so each "presentation" should last no more than ten minutes.

Once you are finished, plan the next session.

DAY 15

Congratulations!

You are at the halfway point in the workbook.

Today, reflect on what this process has been like for you so far.

Talk with each other about what it has been like to spend these half hours with one another, giving undivided, uninterrupted attention.

If, after doing this, you have not used the full thirty minutes, take the extra time to talk about whatever you'd like.

Then plan the next meeting.

DAY 16

Food.

One of my teachers in psychiatry used to say, "Food is love." He was not thin.

Almost all of us love food.

Spend this half hour talking about how food fits into your relationship.

This might lead you to talk about your favorite foods, your favorite restaurants, your most memorable dinner parties, or you might talk about diets and your desire to help each other lose weight, or you might talk about cooking. You might plan some meals, you might decide to change the cooking roles, i.e., who does the cooking and when. You might talk about how food brings you together, or fails to do so.

Before you finish, make plans to eat dinner out together, just the two of you, sometime in the near future.

Then plan the next session.

DAY 17

Foot massage.

Today, give each other a foot massage.

You can do this lying on your bed, or sitting in a chair.

Professionals usually have the client sit in a comfortable chair, while the masseur sits on a stool and holds the client's foot while he gives the massage.

Notice how your conversation varies when you are having your feet rubbed and when you are doing the rubbing.

Don't forget to plan your next present-time session.

DAY 18

Exercise.

Physical exercise is one of the best gifts you can give yourself. It is good for your mind as well as your body.

Today, discuss how you might help each other get more physical exercise.

You might plan to take daily walks together, you might plan to have weekly tennis games together, you might plan to join a health club. I am a member of a health club where a couple comes in regularly to meet with a trainer. You might plan to purchase some exercise equipment for your home.

Exercise happens regularly only if it is scheduled. So, you might plan to help each other set aside time for exercise. Offer encouragement to each other to engage in this hugely beneficial activity.

Don't forget to plan the time and place of your next session.

DAY 19

Give thanks.

Today's exercise is to give thanks.

Take the time together today to look at your lives and give thanks for all that is good. Make an itemized list! You'll be surprised how long it becomes.

Remember the line we cited earlier, "Happiness is not having what you want, it's wanting what you have."

If you spend thirty minutes compiling a list of all that you are grateful for, you will take a giant step toward wanting what you have.

Then plan the next session.

DAY 20

Death.

Ooooh, no, not that.

Yes, that.

It's a bad idea to deny death, then frantically try to deal with it when it is near at hand. And don't say you just hope to die in your sleep. You probably won't.

So, prepare for death.

How you do it is up to you. But do it.

Have a conversation with your mate about death. Thirty minutes on death. Obviously, you can't settle the whole issue in thirty minutes, but you can have a useful and revealing discussion. I'll wager that far from being a bummer, you'll find the conversation actually uplifting.

Then plan the next session.

DAY 21

Today's session is devoted to hopes and dreams.
Ask each other the following question:

*"What would you do if you knew
you could not possibly fail?"*

Then ask each other this question:

*"What would you like us to do as a couple if we knew
we could not possibly fail?"*

Now look at what holds you back from realizing the dreams you just articulated. Usually, it is fear that holds people back, fear masquerading as lack of talent, lack of money, lack of time. If it is fear that is holding you back, try to help each other get past that fear.

Now, plan the next session.

DAY 22

A psychiatrist by the name of Elvin Semrad taught several generations of psychiatrists at Harvard. Even though he wrote little, he survives through those he taught and those they taught, such as Sue and me. Semrad's great subject was the human connection, and his great tool was empathy. He was one of the world's greatest teachers of empathy.

He lives on now through his various sayings, which were all pithy and deceptively simple. For example, he said, "Everyone is either mad, sad, or afraid."

Today, ask each other, "Which are you?"

Maybe you are neither mad, sad, nor afraid. If so, good for you! But if you are somewhat mad, sad, or afraid, discuss these feelings with your partner now.

Then plan the next session.

DAY 23

Today, and for the next three days as well, go up the mountain.

In chapter 7, I mentioned that my wife, Sue, often asks couples to imagine they are sitting at the top of a mountain. She then asks each to describe what they see. Of course, each answer is quite different from the other.

Empathy depends upon knowing the other person's reality. Most people pay lip service to this goal, but they do not do the work it takes to understand the other person's reality.

Today, and for the three days that follow, you will begin that work. You will ask each other four questions, questions you first encountered in chapter 7. Spend the first half of your time on the answer one of you provides, and the second half on the other person's reply.

Today's question is:

"As you look out at your life, what do you see?"

Don't forget to pick the time and place for your next meeting.

DAY 24

Today is the second day looking down from the mountain-top.

Today, ask each other the following question:

"As you look at yourself, what do you see?"

Don't forget to schedule your next meeting.

DAY 25

Day three on the mountain.

Today, ask each other this question:

"As you look at me, what do you see?"

Plan your next session.

DAY 26

Fourth and final day atop the mountain.

Today, ask each other this question:

"As you look at us together, what do you see?"

Don't forget to schedule your next meeting.

DAY 27

After four days on the mountaintop, today we turn to
what you really like. Remember, in the chapter on special-
izing, I said it is important to know what each other really
likes or loves, from an activity to an item to a place, to whatever.

What do each of you truly like or love?

Ask each other that simple question. Try to reply in
depth. What's really fun for you? What do you look forward
to doing? Truly. Not what you wish you looked forward to
doing, not what you think your mate wished you looked forward to doing, but what you honestly look forward to doing.

On some days it could be something as simple as sleep.
On other days, a glass of wine. And on other days . . . you fill
in the blank.

It is helpful for people who are married or living together
to know what the other person considers to be fun and look-
forward-to-able. Then you can special-ize your marriage.

So, explore with each other what you truly love to do,
what you consider to be the most fun activities you know of.

Then plan the next session time.

DAY 28

Money.

Today's topic is money.

No doubt, you've "discussed" this topic with each other before.

Today, you will take a different approach. In keeping with one of the main purposes of this workbook, which is to develop empathy and understanding, I want you each to discuss how you came to have the attitudes, feelings, and behaviors you currently have around money.

Look back to your childhoods. How was money dealt with? What lessons, good and bad, did you learn from your parents and other family members about money?

What did money symbolize in your family?

And what is the emotional meaning of money for each of you now?

Don't discuss finances at all. Just how you came to be the way you are around money now, and what emotions money taps into. For example, for many people money represents basic security. Others measure their self-esteem by how much money they make. And others use money to control and manipulate people. It is a rich topic!

At the end of the session, plan your time for tomorrow.

DAY 29

Sex.

This next-to-last session of the workbook is devoted to sex.

Sex is good. Sex is good for you. Sex is good for your partner.

Today, discuss with your partner what you like about sex between the two of you. Dwell on what you like, don't just skip over it.

Then discuss what you'd like to see change in your sexual experiences with each other. Remember, this is vulnerable territory, so tread lightly, but do try to speak the truth.

Then schedule the next, final session.

DAY 30

You've almost done it! Thirty sessions, thirty days. Congratulations.

Thirty sessions of thirty minutes each of present time, time paying close attention to each other. That's more present time than many couples get in a year, or even in a decade.

The exercise for this final session is first to recount what you've learned. Just say what comes to your mind. What have you learned about each other, about your relationship, and about life during these sessions?

Once you have discussed what you've learned, spend the rest of the session cuddling. Have a glass of wine, if you'd like. Make a toast to your lives together.

And today, and every day, may you reap the many blessings a deep and loving relationship bestows upon you and all you meet.

Acknowledgments

From Ned:

Thanks to friends and colleagues Peter Metz, Michael Thompson, Ken Duckworth, and John Ratey for their many helpful discussions about couples over the years.

I thank Dianne Nargassans and her husband, Robert, a couple who help me day in and day out in planning and developing all that I do. I'd be lost without them!

And I would like to thank three gifted therapists in New York City, Pat Heller, Marcia Stern, and Gillian Walker. Sadly, Marcia died, way too young, while this book was being written. All three of these women taught me not only valuable lessons about couples, but formidable lessons about life.

From Sue:

Thanks to the brilliant and dedicated Corky Becker and the members of the couples' therapy consultation group I have been a part of for years.

Together, our first order of thanks goes to the thousands of couples we have seen in our respective practices over the past twenty-five-plus years. They have taught us the most valuable lessons we've learned. It has been an honor and a privilege to serve the people who have come to us, and we hope they see their contributions throughout this book.

Whenever we are asked where we met, it's fun to be able to say "in a mental hospital." Indeed, Ned was a resident training in psychiatry, and Sue a social worker at the Massachusetts Mental Health Center. We are both grateful to the many teachers one or both of us revered there. To name a few: Tom Gutheil, Doris Benaron, Les Havens, Alan Hobson, Jules Bemporad, Irv Taube, Harry Smith, and George Vaillant.

We also owe thanks to Melissa Orlov, whose name appears on the cover of this book. Melissa helped us through the research she did, the website she oversaw, and the ideas she developed in her own work with couples. She is working on her own book now and we wish her the very best of luck.

We send our thanks and love to Jill Kneerim, Ned's literary agent for lo! these past twenty years. She also came up with the title for this book! Jill is the best agent and friend that we could ask for.

And we thank our editor at Ballantine, Marnie Cochran. Marnie got behind this book from the beginning, and she did what is now rare in publishing: she *improved* the book by editing it, line by line, idea by idea, scene by scene. Her mark is on every page.

Finally, we both thank our children, Lucy, Jack, and Tucker, the lights of our lives, for helping their mom and dad become better parents and better people.

Notes

CHAPTER 1

The study found that being excited and happy S. L. Gable, G. Gonzaga and A. Strachman, "Will You Be There for Me When Things Go Right? Social Support for Positive Events," *Journal of Personality and Social Psychology* 91 (2006): 904–17.

CHAPTER 3

A conservative estimate is that 3 to 6 percent of adult males from "Epidemiology, Prevalence, and Natural History of Compulsive Sexual Behavior;" John M. Kuzma and Donald W. Black; *Psychiatric Clinics of North America* 31 4 (December 2008): 603–11.

ABOUT THE AUTHORS

EDWARD M. HALLOWELL, M.D., was an instructor at Harvard Medical School for twenty years and is now the director of the Hallowell Centers for Cognitive and Emotional Health in Sudbury, Massachusetts, and New York City. He is the co-author of *Delivered from Distraction* and *Driven to Distraction* as well as the author of *CrazyBusy*, *The Childhood Roots of Adult Happiness*, and *Worry*, among other titles.

www.DrHollowell.com

SUE GEORGE HALLOWELL, LICSW, has been a practicing couples' therapist for more than twenty-five years.

The Hallowells are the parents of three teenaged children. They live in Arlington, Massachusetts.